freedom to GROW

ERNEST J. GRUEN

FREEDOM TO GROW

Ernest J. Gruen
Full Faith Church of Love
6824 Lackman Road
Shawnee, Kansas 66217

Copyright © 1983 by Ernest J. Gruen
Printed in the United States of America
ISBN: 0-88368-123-4

All Bible quotations are from the *King James Version* except those identified *NAS* which are from the *New American Standard Bible*, © The Lockman Foundation, 1960, 1962, 1963, 1971, 1972, 1973, 1975, used by permission.

CONTENTS

1. An Appointment with God 7
2. The Benefits Are Mine 18
3. If You Speak It, You Eat It! 29
4. I Believe...Therefore I Speak 39
5. Attempting To Manipulate God 53
6. Goals For Living 64
7. Principles That Work 75
8. Passing Life's Tests 90
9. Encouragement: A Way of Life 105

DEDICATION

To all the loyal, faithful saints of Full Faith Church of Love whose faithfulness is a continual encouragement and blessing to me spiritually.

PREFACE

This book sets forth practical principles on how to live the Christian life. The contents will lead one in how to have a satisfying relationship with the Lord Jesus and also with others. Our Christianity is worthless if it does not help us in our personal relationships.

I wish to express my appreciation, especially, to Bob and Nicki Brunner, who did valuable editing work. Without their labor of love and diligence, the manuscript would not have been released for publication.

Chapter One

An Appointment With God

An overload of thoughts swirled around in my mind while I was driving along the bustling expressway. It was overwhelming—appointments to keep, deadlines to meet, schedules to plan, duties to perform, family commitments, friends in need. The list was endless. So endless, in fact, that my appointment book was full. No free time. I had set up an appointment to either pray with, meet with, or counsel with somebody almost every hour for the next two weeks.

Suddenly, in the recesses of my spirit, the still, small voice of God interrupted my mental busyness. "Son, can *I* have an appointment with you?"

I cried, literally cried, because I was too busy— too busy even for God.

Again, some days later, sitting underneath a tree meditating on the Word, I heard that same quiet voice, "My son, will you obey just one scripture in the Bible? Will you just obey Psalm 63:1, 'Oh, God, thou art my God; early will I seek thee!'? Will you just obey one verse? It's not legalism, it's scripture."

You see, the devil had beguiled and deceived me for many years, because every time I would think about setting aside a consistent time to be with God, Satan's little voice would say, "Legalism! Bondage!" So Satan would trick me out of fellowshipping with my God.

"Oh, God, thou art my God; early will I seek thee: my soul thirsteth for thee, my flesh longeth for thee in a dry and thirsty land, where no water is; To see thy power and thy glory, so as I have seen thee in the sanctuary" (Psalm 63:1-2).

After the Lord revealed this, I began to seriously study Psalm 63. In the second verse it says, "To see thy power and thy glory, so as I have seen thee in the sanctuary." In other words, it says, "I want to see Your power and glory at home, just like I saw it in church on Sunday. Just like I worshipped You in the sanctuary, I want to worship You at home; not just on Sunday morning or Wednesday night. I want to feel Your glory every day."

Now, I'm just as hard-headed as anybody. A few days later, it happened to me a third time. It was three o'clock in the morning, and I couldn't sleep. When I got out of bed to pray, the Lord spoke to my spirit, "In what ways would you like to change your life?" I began to mentally list the things I would like to change. Then the Lord said, "You can change every one of them if you'll just change your schedule. If you'll start each day with an appointment with Me, ninety-five percent of your temptations will cease, and your life, your whole ministry, will fall into divine order. I have told you this before, you've even preached on it, but now it is time for you to do it. If you don't do it, you must resign from the church!"

The next morning I had my first "appointment with God." I call it an appointment with God because that term somehow gets through to me and challenges me. Some call it "quiet time," or "daily devotions," but, although those are good phrases, they somehow don't penetrate my crust. When I use the expression, "I have an appointment with God," that gives it primary importance to me.

I can verify, through personal experience, that *my life has never been any better than my own personal time spent with God*. It doesn't matter what experiences you've had or how long you've been saved, you will never have any better time, more joy, or a more consistent walk with the Lord than you will through your personal appointment with God.

Let me share a little of what a daily appointment with God has done in my life and also in our church.

Each morning I do a live radio broadcast from my home between 7:15 a.m. and 7:30 a.m. Now, I get up at 5:45 a.m., jump in the shower to really wake up, and then spend approximately one hour and 15 minutes praying and reading the Scriptures before that live broadcast. This is my personal appointment with God. When I allow Satan to cheat me out of that time, my whole day seems to be out of orbit. I'm more irritable, more subject to temptation, and I don't flow with people as well. I am sure that this is true for all of us. For example, it is easier for most of us to walk with God during our regular daily routine than when we are on vacation. The reason, obviously, is that we get off schedule and skip our quiet time while on vacation.

There are also daily distractions which try to keep you from your appointment with God. Have you ever noticed, when you're reading the Bible, how Satan reminds you that the car needs a grease job, or that you need to call the beautician for a hair appointment, or that the garbage disposal is broken? We need to take care of those annoyances so that our concentration is on God alone. Often we struggle and fight to dismiss them from our minds. But, you know, I have learned that it *is* possible to let those distractions that Satan meant for evil, work for our good. Our quiet time can organize our day.

During my appointment time with God, I keep a little notepad beside me. When I think I should call a certain person or check on some detail, I make a quick note about it. There are always five or six such things. Once I have jotted them down, I can forget about them and go on with God. Then, after my appointment with God, I have a list of things which I really need to take care of during that day.

Now, sometimes your appointment with God is interrupted by emergencies. Then, as with any other appointment, you have to say, "Well, Lord, because of circumstances, my appointment with You today is going to be for just fifteen minutes instead of an hour." Don't let those times put you under condemnation. God understands emergencies, and He'll look for you to resume your appointment with Him as soon as you can.

In addition to these small distractions, I believe there are five major problems that many people face which tend to come between them and a regular appointment with God. I want to discuss these because I believe that problems are really opportunities to grow. Also, a problem can't be solved until we recognize that it exists. So, if any of these five problems relate to you, praise God, you can now choose to conquer them.

The first problem is *busyness*. We can become so busy doing good things that God is crowded out of our lives. I've talked about some of my busyness and, although you may not quite identify with my life as a pastor, I'm sure you have your own ways of being too busy for God. I have noticed that even lazy people are busy. Have you noticed that? They don't have anything to do, but they keep busy doing it. There is a time principle: a job expands to take up the amount of time available. If you don't have anything to do, you are still busy. Satan will see to it that you're too busy for God.

The second problem is *boredom*. Do you find that you're no longer excited about Jesus? Probably, when you were first saved and filled with the Holy Spirit, you were happy, thrilled and excited. I want to tell you, that if you will schedule a time alone with God every day, that excitement will return to you.

Do you know why you are bored? It isn't the church, and it isn't the preacher. The Bible says, in John 7:38, "He that believeth on me, out of his belly shall flow rivers of living water."

When we were in the land of Israel, we went far enough north to see the source of the Jordan River. Now, everything has a source, right? It has a beginning point. Tell me now, where is the source of a joyful Christian life? The Word says, "Out of your belly shall flow rivers of living water." Tracing it back, it should flow from your innermost being. So, if being bored with God is your problem, then you need to repent and get in your prayer closet with God. It's nobody's fault but your own. You can't pass it off on anyone else because the Bible says the source of your river is from within you. Out of your own belly shall flow rivers of living water.

The third problem that an appointment with God can solve is a *"used to"* relationship with Him.

How do you suppose our wives would react if we said to them, "You know, I used to really love you. I had such a glorious experience with you in the early years of our marriage. It was really wonderful. I really loved you back then."

Brothers, our wives would be crying their eyes out. But then, that's what people often say to God. "You know, I used to really read the Word. I used to really pray. I used to speak in tongues. I used to see people healed. I remember ten years ago...."

You must have an up-to-date, personal relationship with God. Remember, salvation is not just an experience, it is a process, which begins with an experience called the new birth. Since salvation is the *process*, the new birth is simply the gate *into* the process. A daily appointment with God will renew your love relationship with Him.

The fourth problem that an appointment with God will solve is *stagnation*. The problem of stagnation attaches itself just as much to charismatics—those of us who have received the baptism in the Holy Spirit—as any other Christians. You know, we are very susceptible to an infection called a charismatic tapeworm, always listening to the latest cassette, the latest teaching. We are always looking for the newest revelation, the newest teaching that will provide us with a short cut to God. "If I can only get the demons cast out of me."

One man told me in a letter, "I sure hope I have a demon, because if it's a demon, I can get it kicked out of me. But, if it's just me, I don't know what I am going to do."

We are always looking for shortcuts. "If I can just get filled with the Spirit, then I'll be fixed for life." No, you won't!

"If I could just crucify my flesh." "If I can just be water baptized." "If I can just...."

I tell you, the only way that you can have a consistent walk is to have a daily appointment with God. There you can be alone with Him, He can speak to you, and you to Him, and you can get a fresh anointing from God Himself. That's the cure for stagnation.

The fifth problem that is solved by an appointment with God is *formalism or professionalism*.

Every sizable city is full of churches that God once used, where the anointing of the Holy Spirit once was. But now, God only moves in that church every now and then.

I was in a certain city where I was meeting with a pastor whose church had prospered immensely. However, I was deeply disturbed because he wasn't the same man I had known a few years earlier. At the conclusion of the service, which I had preached, he said to me, "Brother Ernie, would you like me to get you out of the sanctuary quickly, so that you won't have to pray with the people?" That really jarred me. I could see that he was starting to just go through the motions.

Now our church in Kansas City has grown to about 2,500 people, which means that we could easily coast for about five years and only be half dead. If you have enough people, you can just begin to slide along, and you don't have to worry. It can become like a perpetual motion machine—coasting and rolling along without the Spirit really moving. It will perpetuate itself for quite a long time. But, I want to tell you that it's a scary thing to wake up to the fact that you're starting to become a professional or just going through a form.

I hate formalism! Do you remember the verse, in 2 Timothy 3:5, which says, "Having a form of godliness, but denying the power thereof?" Horror of horrors, if you don't watch out, one day you're going to find your hands lifted into the air to God, and you won't mean it at all. You'll just be going through the motions. You'll be clapping and singing, but your mind will be on something entirely different from the worship of God. Your heart won't be in it. They will just be motions and rituals—you will have become a formalist.

Now, this pastor who asked me if I wanted to get out of the sanctuary quickly is a dear friend, so I wrote him a letter. Rather than attacking him, I simply told him what God had been telling me. He wrote back and said, "Thank you for your letter of correction. Since I have begun an appointment with God, I am no longer confused and I no longer worry. I am receiving God's direction again for my church."

I began to seek God about formalism in relation to our church. It's a scary thing. I'd hate for you to say of us, "You know, God really used to use that church." What is the answer? The answer isn't to stay small. God doesn't want us to be unsuccessful. God doesn't want just ten saved; He wants thousands saved. I've seen churches of fifty members which have started going through the motions, forms and rituals. I am convinced that the only way we can avoid formalism is to stay on our faces before God. An appointment with God is the only hope for a church, or an individual, to stay out of formalism.

I've been sharing with a number of people what God has put on my heart concerning a daily appointment with Him. In Kansas City we have a city elders meeting, and I began to tell the brothers there about having an appointment with God. I told them not to let anything replace it. Two weeks later, when we met again, one minister said, "I want to thank you, Brother Ernie, for sharing how God dealt with you. In the last two weeks, we have literally seen miracles in our church. Things that we couldn't solve, things there were no answers for, problems that looked as if they would bring division, suddenly worked out. I even have all kinds of extra time since I have been having an appointment with God every day." He continued, "I have done it twelve out of fourteen days, and I have seen its power. I also know how important it is because I can see how I act and how I feel when I miss a day."

Another pastor called me. He said, "I heard about your church. I need help. Can you help me?"

I said, "Brother, do you have an appointment with God?"

"What are you talking about?" he asked, puzzled.

I began to explain it to him. Within ten minutes he said to me, "That is the answer. I know what I need to do."

The same is true for you, my reader. Let me tell you very kindly, if you don't make up your mind to have an appointment with God, you'll end up being bored and stagnant, regardless of how much God has used you in the past. This isn't optional.

Begin your own daily appointment with God. It is the very key to your spiritual growth, to being a successful Christian, consistent in your love, devotion and obedience to the Lord Jesus Christ. If you will do it, believe me, it will revolutionize your life!

Chapter Two

The Benefits Are Mine

So, now we have established an appointment with God. And we have done it because of *who* He is and how much we *love* Him. I don't know about you, but I truly miss God's presence when I find myself drawing away from Him.

Even though we don't pursue time with God for the personal benefits, I have found that He is faithful to His Word and rewards us just the same. There are at least seven wonderful benefits that are ours through establishing an appointment with God. You will undoubtedly find even more.

Number one: *right priorities.* You will never get your priorities right until your priority with God is right.

Now, let me explain: if you keep your appointment with God, you will have time for your family. Life's proper priorities are God first, spouse and children second, and business third. Now, you may understand that, but do you do it? When you make up your mind that, no matter what, you are going to meet with God every day, then you will suddenly find that you are a natural, loving, caring spouse. You will have more time to spend with your family.

When you are a dull axe, you have to swing fifty times to chop down a tree. A sharp axe gets the job done quickly, and with ease. For example, when people come in for counseling now, the Holy Spirit quickly points His finger to the problem, and the problems are solved in one third the time. Why? Because I have been with Jesus that day. Instead of a three hour drudgery, because I wasn't a sharp axe, because I was living and counseling out of yesterday's experience, we get to the root of the problem quickly. And we can work with success from there. When you get in the Spirit, and get your priority with God right, the amazing thing is that you don't have to worry about the other priorities. They fall into place.

Benefit number *two* is that *guilt is lifted*. Previously, when I didn't get into the Word of God during the morning, I found that when I came home at night I had trouble reading the newspaper, or being human with the family, because of feelings of guilt that I should be studying the Word. I couldn't play a game or be natural with my children because I felt guilty about what I hadn't done—what I should have done—at the beginning of the day. The amazing thing, now, is that I can come home and read the newspaper without guilt. Why? Because I have put first things first and have spent time with God early in the day. I can even watch Monday Night Football if I want. Before, I felt guilty about it. Now, I can do some of those natural things that may not seem important, but allow you to relax and enjoy life. The guilt is gone.

A *third* benefit of an appointment with God is that it will *eliminate about ninety-five percent of your temptations.*

When you get alone with God every morning, you will find that you are no longer irritable, crabby and grouchy. You will no longer have problems with dirty thoughts or lust. A man said to me, "I am having a terrible time with lustful thoughts." I told him, "Let's not look at the problem, let's look at the solution. Instead of trying to stop sinning, why don't you start Godding?" Don't focus on the sin. Focus on God. Why should you waste your time attacking a problem? Put your efforts into the solution.

Try an experiment with me. Think of the White House, just visualize it in your mind.

Okay, now stop thinking about the White House. Don't give it another thought. Do you see? You can't, because you are concentrating on not thinking about the White House.

Now think about a beautiful orange tree covered with oranges. See? Some of the oranges have fallen off. There now, you forgot all about the White House, didn't you?

The point is, if you try, for example, to stop lusting, if you say to yourself, "I am not going to lust," you're already thinking about lusting in your mind. You, in effect, tempt yourself. So when the man said, "I am having a terrible time with lustful thoughts," I said to him, "Forget about your problems. Just get alone with God." When I talked to this man later and asked how he was doing, he said, "Ever since I have had my appointment with God, I don't have any more problems with lustful thoughts."

Sometimes we can be pretty dense. Counseling can be problem-centered. Jesus is solution-centered.

Benefit number *four* of an appointment with God is that *your day will become organized*.

Now I have preached an appointment with God for more than two years in our church. I don't always preach a whole sermon on it, but whenever I find a verse that fits it, I mention it. Why? Because when we get hold of a truth, we tend to think, "Well, I have learned that, and it's taken care of." But God doesn't want just a sermon on it. He wants this message planted in the spirit of everyone who hears it, until it grows to be a part of them.

Since I have been planting the message of an appointment with God in our church, people have been coming to me saying, "Ever since I have been having an appointment with God, I get so much more done. Everything falls into place. My day has become organized. I get the housework done in record time," or, "I get more work done on the job than I have ever done before."

It's true! Try it yourself and see. The whole day falls into place when you start it with God.

Benefit number *five* is, *it will affect those around*

you.

My secretary came to me and said, "Brother Ernie, I don't understand it, but suddenly this office is not as chaotic as it was before." It was true. The atmosphere of the whole church office had changed, and confusion had left all those around me. Three of the associate pastors came to me and said, "Since you have been having your appointment with God, we are under so much conviction that we have been doing it, too."

Members of the congregation came to me and said, "Ernie, we have noticed that your preaching is more penetrating now. It was good before, but now it is really getting through to me."

A *sixth* benefit is that *it will have an effect on your family.*

In the middle of the night, God told me, "The only one that needs to change in your family is you." See? Christianity is caught—not taught. Do you understand that?

Suppose I have chicken pox and say to you, "I have the measles." Then I give you a complete description of measles: the incubation period, the signs and symptoms, the fever—an eloquent description.

But, you are still going to catch chicken pox, not measles. You are going to get what I got, not what I taught.

You can tell your kids, "I love Jesus; Jesus is my Lord." Still, they are going to catch what you are, not what you teach. Your family sees what you are. The one who needs to change is you. When your family sees the change in you from your appointment with God, they'll want what you have.

A *seventh* benefit is that *deliverance from demons* comes from an appointment with God.

John 8:31-32 says, "If you continue in My word, then are you My disciples indeed; and you shall know the truth, and the truth shall make you free."

It says, "If you continue in My word, you shall know the truth." The only way to know the truth is to continue in the Word, and then, that truth shall set you free. In reference to demons, Matthew 8:16 says, ". . . He cast out the spirits with His word. . . ." His Word will free you from demons. You will know the truth, and the truth shall set you free—if you continue in the Word. Get in the Word through a daily appointment with God.

Now, let me make some practical suggestions as to how to establish your daily appointment. *Number one*, do you have thirty minutes a day for God? May I suggest that if you do not have thirty minutes a day for God, then God is not your God.

You say, "Jesus is my Lord."

"Oh, really? Do you have thirty minutes a day for Him?"

"I don't have time."

If you have put aside daily time to be with the Lord, then in a very practical way, He is becoming your Lord.

Suggestion *number two,* remember the scripture we gave you earlier, Psalm 63:1, says, "Early will I seek thee." To the Jews, and in the Bible, a day begins at 6:00 p.m. and ends at the next sunset. In our culture, we consider a day to begin when the sun rises. So then, biblically speaking, the verse, "Early will I seek thee" means that the earliest we could seek God on any day is 6:01 p.m. Now, the reason I bring up this point is that we are all different and have different schedules. Some of us are early birds, and some of us are night owls. It makes no difference to God whether you schedule your appointment late at night or early the next morning. The important thing is, do it!

Here is a *third* suggestion. There are thirty-one chapters in the book of Proverbs. Most of us in our church regularly read the Proverb of the day. If it's the 15th of the month, we read Proverbs, the 15th chapter. In that way we read through Proverbs once each month, with its very practical rules for living. Then, we go to whatever other section of the Bible we are currently studying. It's a good way to begin each appointment.

A *fourth* suggestion is that you buy a loose-leaf notebook. Why? As an example, during last month's trip through Proverbs, I kept, on each page, two parallel columns. One column was headed "evil mouth," and the second column was headed "righteous mouth." As I read, I wrote down every reference to the tongue. Interestingly, there is more in Proverbs about a righteous mouth, than about an evil one. I now have a record about that aspect of teaching in Proverbs. I'll add to the listings as I come upon other references in other books of the Bible concerning the mouth.

There are many other such study topics which are easily discerned for study in your trips through Proverbs, or through Psalms, etc: Truth about the wise versus the foolish, the wicked versus the upright, the sluggard versus the worker. Digging into God's Word makes being alone with God exciting. A brother came to me after church recently. He said, "Ever since I got a notebook, the Bible is a brand new book. I bring my notebook to church with me, and take notes whenever I hear the Holy Spirit speaking through the teacher or the preacher. It forces me to concentrate. I get twice as much out of the messages." He continued, "I use a loose-leaf binder so that I can reorganize it by topics." Try it. It helps you concentrate, and meditate; it delivers you from daydreaming, makes the Word exciting, and lets you review the teachings at will.

Now here is suggestion number *five*, pray-read Scripture. One day as I was reading the Bible, God said, "Don't just read it, pray it." That has revolutionized both my Bible study and my life. For example, if you read, "Jacob blessed his children," you immediately stop and bless your kids. "Lord, bless my son with the spirit of joy. Lord, bless my daughter with the spirit of encouragement." If you read in Psalm 144 about no complaining in the streets, say, "Lord, I choose to quit complaining in the streets, or at home, or anywhere." Whatever you read, pray it into your spirit. As you read about David committing adultery with Bathsheba, say, "God, in Jesus' name, help me to never be so foolish and so disloyal to my commitments to You and to my wife (or husband)." If you read a reproaching scripture, pray that you will never do such a thing. As you read a positive verse, ask God to help you be that way. As you read, different verses will remind you of different people. Pray that scripture for them. Suddenly, the Bible becomes your prayer book, and your prayers make your Bible reading exciting.

As an introduction to the *sixth* suggestion, I'll tell you the story of how it was introduced to me.

I was on an out-of-town speaking engagement and sharing a room with another pastor and close brother in the Lord named Harry. We were in our room, each doing his own study and meditation. I looked over at Harry and saw that he was reading a book on church history. A few minutes later, I noticed that he was studying Greek grammar. Then, a bit later, he was reading biblical archeology.

"Harry," I asked, "what are you doing?"

He replied, "I read in *Reader's Digest* that executives have found that, by spending ten minutes a day reading any book on an auxiliary or parallel field to their occupation, they can become experts in that field. Just ten minutes a day, over a period of time, does it. I spend ten minutes a day reading church history, ten minutes studying Greek, and ten minutes on biblical archeology." That's how I came upon my last suggestion, which I call the "ten-minutes-a-day" principle. I thought, "my goodness, if the world can do that for money, surely we can do it for the Lord." I want to say that the results are clearly evident when Harry preaches. Information and knowledge just flow out of him.

I have had, for years, a fifteen-hundred page church history book on my office shelf. I've wanted to read it, but, wow! fifteen hundred pages! I can't do that! But, if you have a ten-minutes-a-day principle, you can read that church history for ten minutes and put it back on the shelf. I have already preached two sermons from thoughts taken out of that church history book. It has broadened my knowledge and given me new understanding, just by ten minutes a day.

We have taught this principle in our church: spend thirty minutes a day with God. Then, spend ten minutes in Halley's Bible Handbook, or whatever book the Holy Spirit leads you to. One of the benefits is that if, in the future, someone comes with a new revelation, or some weird doctrine, it will spark a remembrance in you to say, "Hey, that's nothing but the same kind of controversy that occurred in the early church."

As I was thinking about this, I saw, in my mind's eye, a vision of a concrete floor being poured, with reinforcing rods in it. Too often we try to build our foundation and our walls without any steel in them. Without reinforcement, our foundations will chip or crumble with the first storm.

Make your decision to have an appointment with God every day, and to broaden your knowledge through spending ten minutes each day in a book the

Holy Spirit leads you to. Suddenly, you'll find yourself becoming a Christian with some backbone and some steel reinforcement in you. You'll find yourself becoming the one who is called on for help, rather than the one calling out for help.

Here is a familiar verse out of God's Word: "So shall my word be that goeth forth out of my mouth: it shall not return unto me void, but it shall accomplish that which I please, and it shall prosper in the thing whereto I sent it" (Isaiah 55:11).

If you get into the Word of God every day, God promises you that His Word is not going to return void in your life. It is going to prosper inside of you. It is going to accomplish something for you. When you get the Word in you, it is a seed, and it explodes in you as new life. The Word of God will not prove void for you. It is going to accomplish and prosper within you.

Here is another verse, "Blessed is the man who listens to me, watching daily at my gates, waiting at my doorposts. For he who finds me finds life, and obtains favor from the Lord" (Proverbs 8:34-35, *NAS*). I like that phrase, "watching daily." Do you want to find favor with God? Then watch daily. Set up a daily appointment with God. You will be on the road to becoming an excited, joyful, anointed, consistent, mature Christian. You will enjoy your new freedom to grow in Him!

Chapter Three

If You Speak It, You Eat It!

Are you teachable? Are you willing to grow?

Then listen to what you read here, meditate on its meaning for you, and practice the teaching diligently. God will nurture it within you!

The Lord has been showing me how important it is that I don't just preach. He wants me to plant. Seeds don't grow very well when you just scatter them about, one here, one there. You need to plant them properly in good soil to see real growth. The same thing holds true with God's people. We have the freedom to grow spiritually to heights beyond what we have ever imagined. God wants to see us grow strong spiritually in Him and in His ways. But we need to have His Word planted deeply in our spirits.

In my own pastorate, God has given me certain teachings that He wants to plant in the spirits of His people. One of those teachings I have already shared with you: the vital need for an appointment with God. There is another teaching that is also very important to our growth; that is *mouth confession*.

Over a period of several months, the Lord has led me to keep emphasizing these things; keep teaching them until it's no longer a sermon, until our people begin to think on, act on, live out, manifest, and do the things being taught. I have begun to perceive that when the Holy Spirit moves in a certain direction, one sermon won't be adequate to cover it. It takes a series of messages, teachings, and emphasis until finally everyone begins to speak and act out what the Holy Spirit is saying to the church at that time.

Let's get into the subject of mouth confession by looking first at Scripture.

"A man's belly shall be satisfied with the fruit of his mouth; and with the increase of his lips shall he be filled. Death and life are in the power of the tongue: and they that love it shall eat the fruit thereof" (Proverbs 18:20-21).

Let's look at that scripture phrase by phrase. "A man's belly shall be satisfied with the fruit of his mouth." In other words, we spread the table of our lives by what we speak with our mouths. Whatever you speak with your mouth, you have to eat it. If you speak failure, defeat, negativism or depression, you have to eat that all day long. "A man's belly shall be satisfied with the fruit of his mouth."

If you eat a hamburger, it becomes a part of you. When you eat natural food with your mouth, it becomes part of your body. In the same context, this verse is saying that what you speak with your mouth becomes part of your spirit. *You feed your spirit by what you speak with your mouth.* Now, if you live by that principle, it will revolutionize your life. Some of us have confessed defeat, talked failure, spoken self-condemnation for so long that we have broken our spirit and *conditioned ourselves to defeat, failure and depression by our own mouths.*

The next phrase says, "And with the increase of his lips shall he be filled." What is meant by "the increase of his lips"? That doesn't mean that our lips really get bigger! It means that we begin to change what we speak from our lips. We begin to say, "Praise the Lord, Jesus is in me! Life is going to flow out of me. Love is going to flow from my words. This is the day that the Lord has made. I will rejoice and be glad in it! Whoever touches me today is going to touch God, because the Spirit of God is in me! Whoever touches my life is going to be made happy and joyful. I'm going to minister life to people today. My family is going to be happy. The anointing of God is on me!"

When we begin to talk like that, we begin to increase what we speak. We begin to create by what we say. When something is created, it represents an increase. "With the increase of his lips shall he be filled."

"A man's belly shall be satisfied with the fruit of his mouth"; what he speaks then is creative and fulfilling. "And with the increase of his lips shall he be filled," filled with God, filled with the Holy Spirit.

We each need to start confessing, "God is going to use me today. There is going to be someone healed through my life today. Someone will be healed in their mind today. There's a river of life flowing out through me. It makes the lame to walk and the blind to see. It opens prison doors and sets the captive free. There's a river of life flowing out through me!"

You may think that's pride, but that is faith. The Holy Spirit is inside of you if you're a born-again Christian. God the Father, God the Son, and God the Holy Spirit are in you. But, more than that, whoever touches you is going to touch the very Spirit of God.

Now let's look at the next verse: "Death and life are in the power of the tongue." That's quite a scripture. In other words, we minister to ourselves, either life or death, by what we speak. You can speak yourself into victory, or, you can speak yourself into depression. You minister life or death to yourself, to your own spirit, to your own personality, by what comes out of your mouth.

Not only does this affect you, but you also minister either life or death to those around you by what you speak. You minister to your spouse. You minister to your children. You minister to your friends. You minister to those you work with. They will sense what flows out of you.

I have recently read a book written by Bob Buess entitled, *Favor, the Road to Success.** This excellent Christian book contains testimonies which illustrate

---

**Favor, the Road to Success,* Bob Buess, P.O. Box 7110, Tyler, TX 75711. Used by permission.

the truth that others do sense your spirit. In it, Bob Buess relates the story of a young woman who was applying for a secretarial job. The employer was looking for full-time help, but she could only work for three months during the summer. She had already confessed God's favor concerning this interview.

The employer read her application and then turned to her and said, "Why do you think I should hire you?"

"I am a blessing everywhere I go," was her response. "I am a blessing to my employer," she continued.

He said, "I need a full-time, permanent girl. I can't understand why, since you only have three months to work, but I'm hiring you."

She stayed with the job for the three months, and her boss was very pleased with her. When the time came for her to leave, the employer said to her, "Can you find someone else who is so full of life and victory to replace you? I have never had such a pleasant experience with an employee."

Now, that's Christianity in action! She confessed, she believed, she went in by faith and came out with that job.

In that same book is the testimony of another positive confession. A middle-aged woman named Jane had come to Bob Buess confessing that she needed a job. Her problems were many; she hadn't held a job for ten years; she was a poor typist; and no one would want to hire an older woman over a younger woman.

He talked with Jane about her confession and encouraged her to confess favor and success with the job interview scheduled a few days off. She did change her confession. She faithfully spoke success into her spirit. She claimed Daniel 1:9 as her confession; "Now God granted Daniel favor and compassion in the sight of the commander of the officials." She became excited about her prospects.

You guessed it. Jane got the job. The employer said, "I was going to hire someone else, but for reasons I don't quite understand, I've decided to hire you."

Later, Jane came back to Bob Buess saying that although she appreciated the job, "It's a rat race. The office is full of confusion. The staff is overworked. The demands are more than can be accomplished."

Together, they began to confess peace, favor, success, and harmony for the whole office. Soon it happened. They reorganized the entire office and brought in all new desks for everyone but Jane. For her, they provided a small office to herself where she could be away from all the confusion of the outer office. She found herself with just the right amount of work; at times she would even relieve the other girls by doing some of their work. There was no earthly explanation for her to have found such favor.

Do those testimonies speak the spirit of faith to you? They do to me. Change your confession. Increase your confession. Confess that you are going to be successful and prosperous from all kinds of sources.

I made the confession of prosperity the other day when I had some financial needs. Within twelve hours someone walked up to me and said, "Here, the Lord told me to give you this." They gave me sixty dollars! The Lord answered so quickly I could hardly grasp it. As soon as possible, I gave ten dollars of that money away; I've planted it to help somebody else. Hallelujah! "Death and life are in the power of the tongue."

"Now if we put the bits into the horses' mouths so that they may obey us, we direct their entire body as well. Behold, the ships also, though they are so great and are driven by strong winds, are still directed by a very small rudder, wherever the inclination of the pilot desires. So also the tongue is a small part of the body, and yet it boasts of great things..." (James 3:3-5, *NAS*).

The Word says that the tongue is like the horse's bit. It's like the rudder on a ship. Even when the waves are big and the winds are strong, it is the rudder that determines the direction of the ship.

Do you catch the principle? *Your tongue will determine the direction of your entire life.* Your tongue is the rudder of your life. The circumstances will not determine your direction, but your mouth's response to your circumstances will determine your direction and destiny. You speak, and what you say with your mouth-rudder will determine whether you'll be happy, successful and prosperous, or defeated, negative and feeling inferior.

It depends upon your tongue and what you speak. Your tongue is the rudder that controls your vessel, regardless of how fierce the storm you face. Now quit yielding to the storm. Start believing God and speaking success with your mouth. You *can* determine the direction of your life.

I want to talk, just a bit now, about negative confession. Satan's plan is negativism. *Satan wants you sick, sad, sinful, and expecting worse!* Satan expects you to play right into his hands.

"For the thing which I greatly feared is come upon me, and that which I was afraid of is come unto me" (Job 3:25).

I know of a spiritual leader who is a servant of God and has been mightily used of God. But he has gotten into negativism. He talks defeat, believes in defeat, expects defeat, and has begun to receive it. In his publications, he has begun to complain about his fears for his ministry, his offices, his own safety. He's a valued brother, and I've written him, in love, pointing out that Satan has tricked him into believing fears.

I read, in a published survey concerning women who have been sexually assaulted, that most of these women had a deep fear, prior to their attack, that they would be assaulted. It seems that a rapist can sense the spirit of fear in a woman.

You women ought to say, "Blessed be God, I'm under His protection. I'm in the secret place. I'm abiding in Christ. No harm is going to come nigh me.

I claim Psalm 91: 'He that dwelleth in the secret place of the most High shall abide under the shadow of the Almighty.'" The Lord's protection is better than a can of mace.

A couple of years ago, a sister in our church was carrying out trash from her apartment when a man jumped out and grabbed her to assault her. She said, "In the name of Jesus Christ let me go." That man dropped her and took off like a scared rabbit. The Bible promises us, "The name of the Lord is a strong tower; The righteous runs into it and is safe" (Proverbs 18:10, *NAS*).

And, as we get older, we need to become more alert about becoming negative. Older saints, many times, read the newspapers for every assault, every murder, every weird happening—looking for all the negatives. Then they begin to say, "My, my, what's the world coming to? It didn't used to be like this. Oh dear, secular humanism is taking over."

That is a demonic spirit of negativism and unbelief. The things that you think about, speak with your lips, and worry about, are going to show up at your front door. It's Satan's pattern of defeatism. If you think you're a failure, and confess doubt and fear so long that you believe it, your mind is conditioned to failure. You accept failure and get comfortable in it. You get defeatism into your spirit and you're under condemnation.

You need to rebel against that whole pattern of defeat. Rebel against the negative faith, faith in failure. Begin to confess "Hallelujah! I'm loved! I'm prosperous! I'm one of God's kids! The anointing is on me! I abide under the shadow of the Almighty! There is life coming out of me! I'm going to cheer somebody up today!" Don't be captured by defeat. Be captured by faith.

Chapter Four

I Believe...
Therefore I Speak

Faith is an essential part of mouth confession. Without faith, what we are speaking is just a lot of words.

"But having the same spirit of faith, according to what is written, 'I believed, therefore I spoke,' we also believe, therefore also we speak" (2 Corinthians 4:13, *NAS*).

Paul says we believe and *therefore* we speak. That leads me to the conclusion that faith is more than just a heart thing. Faith is a heart *and* a mouth thing. Faith is speaking what you *believe*. A miracle requires two things: heart faith and mouth confession. "For verily I say unto you, That whosoever shall say unto this mountain, Be thou removed, and be thou cast into the sea; and shall not doubt in his heart, but shall believe that those things which he saith shall come to pass; he shall have whatsoever he saith" (Mark 11:23).

Some people don't like teaching on mouth confession because they think it might mean confessing a lie. But notice how accurate the Scriptures are, "According to what is written, I believe." That means that *the Bible is your confession book*. When the Bible says, for example, "I can do all things through Christ which strengthens me," you can depend on it as being the truth *because it has been written*. "According to what is *written,* I *believe,* and therefore I *speak*."

So there are really three steps in a godly mouth confession: 1. *Find out what is written,* 2. *Believe it,* and then 3. *Speak it.*

You can do all things through Christ which strengthens you.

"Then said Mary unto the angel, 'How shall this be, seeing I know not a man?' And the angel answered and said unto her, 'The Holy Ghost shall come upon thee, and the power of the Highest shall overshadow thee: therefore also that holy thing which shall be born of thee shall be called the Son of God. And, behold, thy cousin Elizabeth, she hath also conceived a son in her old age: and this is the sixth month with her, who was called barren. For with God nothing shall be impossible!" (Luke 1:34-37). This is literally translated, "with God *no word* shall be impossible."

God worked a double miracle. First with Elizabeth who was too old to conceive, and then with Mary who had not known a man. The angel said, in effect, "After all, nothing God has spoken by His word is impossible!"

"But," you say, "I know God performs miracles

and that nothing is impossible with Him. But it's me and my needs that I'm concerned about."

"Then came the disciples to Jesus apart, and said, Why could we not cast him out? And Jesus said unto them, Because of your unbelief: for verily I say unto you, If ye have faith as a grain of mustard seed, ye shall say unto this mountain, Remove hence to yonder place; and it shall remove; and nothing shall be impossible unto you" (Matthew 17:19-20).

Did you get that? Jesus said that nothing shall be impossible *unto you!* And what did Jesus mean by, "faith as a grain of mustard seed"? He is saying that faith starts as a seed. It doesn't start as a tree. It has to be planted.

I would like to plant in you, faith, joy and encouragement. Now, it starts small, but it grows. We begin with faith as a grain of mustard seed.

Let me illustrate. I used to have migraine headaches, and they were excruciating. I knelt in front of a bathroom stool holding my head, thinking that every blood vessel in my head was going to break. I was praying to vomit in order to be rid of the migraine. But one day, after I had been filled with the Holy Spirit, I began to have faith that Jesus could heal me. I read in the Word, "He Himself took our infirmities, and carried away our diseases" (Matthew 8:17, *NAS*). Faith was growing in my heart.

Then one day, I said, "I do not have to have these headaches." Now that was just a seed, but I turned a corner as soon as I said, "I don't have to have these."

That's faith as a grain of mustard seed. After that point, even though I still didn't have victory over them, I no longer believed that I had to keep them. "Therefore you believe, and so you speak." I read God's Word on healing; the seed of faith was planted; it began to grow; and I began to take a stand against those headaches. I began to fight against them. I began to say, "I won't accept them. I won't believe in them." They began to lessen in intensity! They began to lessen in frequency, until, now I don't have them. But it was a definite battle.

Jesus says that faith grows. So plant a seed of faith in your spirit. Read the Bible, "His name will be called Wonderful, Counselor, the Mighty God, the Everlasting Father, the Prince of Peace" (Isaiah 9:6). Then say, "I don't need to smoke! I don't have any use for cigarettes! He is my Mighty God! I don't need to have something always in my fingers to calm my nerves. I'm not nervous! I have the Prince of Peace with me! He's all I need!" Now you may smoke for another six months, but the devil is on the way to being defeated because the seed of faith is in you. It's growing, and it's going to grow and grow until the desire to smoke is out of you. The same principle applies to a bad temper or lustful thoughts. Once you see in God's Word that you don't have to have that temper or those thoughts, then the seed has been planted. It begins to grow as you begin to believe it and then confess it.

"Therefore you believe, and so you speak," and God begins to increase your faith. That seed of faith grows, and one day you wake up and, glory to God, the mountain has moved! You have found out that nothing is impossible to you. You can change. You can be clean. You can be pure. You can have peace.

"And the glory which Thou hast given Me I have given to them; that they may be one, just as We are one" (John 17:22, *NAS*). He gives us His glory in order that we might have unity, one with another.

"And whom He predestinated, these He also called; and whom He called, these He also justified; and whom He justified, these He also glorified" (Romans 8:30, *NAS*).

Notice the tense. He says he's already called us, already justified us, and already glorified us. Dear friend, you're not going to get glory, you've already been glorified if you're in Christ Jesus. You need to begin to confess that. It's the Word, and "according as it is written, I believe and therefore I speak."

Confess that the glory of God is on you.

Confess that the Spirit of the Lord is upon you.

Confess that God's countenance is upon your countenance.

"And the Lord spake unto Moses, saying, Speak unto Aaron, and unto his sons, saying, On this wise ye shall bless the children of Israel, saying unto them, The Lord bless thee and keep thee: The Lord make His face shine upon thee, and be gracious unto thee: The Lord lift up His countenance upon thee, and give thee peace" (Numbers 6:22-26).

Do you realize that this blessing, given by God to the children of Israel, belongs to you and me as well?

That's what His Word says, and His Word is true. In the eleventh chapter of Romans it says that through Jesus Christ we, as gentiles, are grafted into Israel, the chosen people of God. And again, in Ephesians 2:19, we are promised that we have been made members of the household of God.

So, the blessings God gave Moses to give to His children apply to us.

Believe it! That's faith in the heart. *Confess it!* That's faith from the mouth.

"I am blessed of the Lord God."

"He is keeping me. I don't have to sin."

"The Lord is making His face to shine upon my face. I'm shining, right now!"

"The glory of the Lord is upon me."

"He is being gracious unto me."

"He is lifting up my countenance."

"He is blessing me with peace."

"I have the smile of Jesus on my face."

Now, I want you to imagine that a great spotlight is moving across the room where you're reading this. It's searching for the one whom God wants to bless. Now that spotlight lands right on you, and God is saying to you, "Stand up! I really love you! I am going to bless you and prosper you and use you! I'm going to flow through you! My face shines on you! My peace is in you, just you! You are chosen of God! My spotlight is on you!"

In Bob Buess' book, *Favor, the Road to Success*, he points out that Jesus had favor. It says in the Gospel of Luke that when Jesus was a child, He grew in stature, in wisdom, and in favor before God and man. Jesus, in fact, had so much favor that he practically had to insult Pilate to get Himself crucified. Just think how easy it would have been for Jesus to get out of the crucifixion. Instead, Jesus chose to follow God's will.

Bob Buess shares several other exciting examples of God's favor in our lives. There were two young children who were having problems with low grades in school. Their mother decided to confess with them daily from Luke 2:40. "Jesus grew and waxed strong in spirit, filled with wisdom; and the grace of God was upon Him." Then she had each of them repeat the verse using his own name, saying, "I am growing in the Lord. I am waxing strong in spirit. I am learning new wisdom today. I have favor with God and with my teachers and with my fellow schoolmates."

On their next report cards, one went from an F to a C. The other went from a D to a B. They confessed their way up two grade points just by changing their mouth confession.

In another instance, a man was going to be called-on-the-carpet for holding lunchtime Bible studies in an empty room at work. Before he went in to see the boss, he prayed, "I confess to you, God, that I am going to find favor with that boss. He's going to love me, and I'm going to love him. When he meets me, he's going to meet the Spirit of God."

When he went to the office, the boss started to chew him out. He said, "I understand you've been holding Bible studies in that empty room."

"That's right," he replied. "I certainly have."

Within a few minutes of his discussion, that boss was so overwhelmed by the Spirit of God that he said, "I'll get you chairs, songbooks and a piano for that room."

Most of us have been living in defeat for too long. We've been discounting the love, favor and power of our God far too long. It's time to change our confession.

A charismatic couple was beginning to develop a persecution complex. "Nobody likes us in our church since we've become Spirit-filled," they claimed. "They relieved my husband from being Sunday school superintendent. They won't let me teach my class any more," said the wife.

When they sought outside advice, they were told to quit expecting bad things and to begin confessing good things. This couple changed their confession and began to confess God's favor, expect God's favor and believe in success.

They said it was almost embarrassing. They were like magnets in church. People seemed to be drawn to them. They became the hub of activities. Things seemed to flow around them, just because they started making the right confessions based on their faith.

You see, as a Christian, by making right mouth confessions, you can change bad situations into good situations. Don't let yourself just yield to your environment.

Think of the experiences and situations confronting Joseph in the book of Genesis. Can you imagine what it did to a seventeen year old boy to be sold at an auction in Egypt? What would that have done to your spirit?

"Who'll give me 20, 20, 20! Here's 20! 21, 21, 21, here! Hey, 23, 24, give me 25, hey, 25, sold. Hebrew slave boy sold to Potiphar for 25 coins."

If we had been standing there, we would have wept. A foreigner in a strange land, sold into slavery. But Joseph was full of God, and it wasn't long before he was running the whole household of Potiphar.

Then Joseph was framed for adultery, of which he was absolutely innocent. He was thrown into jail anyway. But the Bible says that he found favor with the jailor. Soon he was running the jail. But even more amazing, after spending only an hour with the Pharoah, he was running the whole nation of Egypt!

What was it that Joseph had? It sure wasn't negativism. That's for certain. He must have said, "Hallelujah! I may be in jail, but I'm ruling. Glory to God!"

It was the same with Daniel. The Bible says in Daniel 1:9 that Daniel found God's favor, and it wasn't long before he went from a captive to ruler over Babylon.

I want you to grasp something here. *I want you to grasp a way of life*, a way of speaking, a way of living. I want you to understand that all things are possible to you, if you believe and speak it. I want to sow a seed of faith in you. I want you to understand that your tongue is your rudder, and that it will determine the whole direction of your life. I want you to understand that life and death are in the power of your tongue.

Now, take a look at Paul. He was put in jail. He shouted, sang and praised his way out of one jail, but he wrote a large part of the Bible while he was in another one. In both the jail he was delivered from, and the jail he had to stay in, Paul ruled the situation. He didn't let the situation rule him.

If you're in a bad situation, you can still believe right and confess right. Maybe God won't let you get out of some situation you think He should free you from. You just stay where the Lord has you and be full of love, joy, peace and the Holy Spirit, with the glory of God on your countenance, and God will do something great for you. Or, He will make something great come out of the situation.

Some of you who read this have what I call billy-goat faith, "Yes, but-but-but-but-but." So now I want to speak to the "yes-buts."

"Yes, but I have a lower mental ability than some. I don't have an I.Q. of 120."

"God hath chosen the foolish things of the world to confound the wise.... But of him are ye in Christ Jesus, who of God is made unto us wisdom, and righteousness, and sanctification, and redemption" (1 Corinthians 1:27, 30).

"Yes, but I feel rejected."

"Now therefore ye are no more strangers and foreigners, but fellow citizens with the saints, and of the household of God" (Ephesians 2:19).

Just stop and confess that scripture aloud. "I am not a stranger. I'm not a foreigner. I am a fellow citizen with the saints, and I am of the household of God."

Didn't that feel good? Now do it again. Then add, "I am not rejected. I'm part of God's in-group. I'm born of the Spirit of God. God is my father. Jesus is my brother. The Holy Spirit is my constant companion. I am not left out. I have been included in the Kingdom of God. I'm God's child."

"Yes, but I'm handicapped."

"The lame take the prey" (Isaiah 33:23).

That's God's Word. He says, "The lame take the prey." If you're handicapped, use it. You can take the prey.

"Yes, but I am weak."

"Hast thou not known? Hast thou not heard, that the everlasting God, the Lord, the Creator of the ends of the earth, fainteth not, neither is weary? There is no searching of his understanding. He giveth power to the faithful; and to them that have no might he increaseth strength" (Isaiah 40:28-29). "Even the youths shall faint and be weary, and the young men shall utterly fall: But they that wait upon the Lord shall renew their strength; they shall mount up with wings as eagles; they shall run, and not be weary; and they shall walk, and not faint." (Notice that this verse mentions the appointment with God as the key to success!)

"Yes, but I am untrained."

"I was no prophet, neither was I a prophet's son;

but I was a herdsman, and a gatherer of sycamore fruit: and the Lord took me..." (Amos 7:14-15).

"*Yes, but* I will make a mistake."

"Where no oxen are, the crib is clean..." (Proverbs 14:4). I'd better stop and explain that one. Being a Kansas farm boy, that's one of my favorite verses. Oxen were essential on the farm for getting any work done. But if you had oxen working in the field, then you had oxen living in the stable, and you had to feed them, care for them, and clean up after them. It wasn't always the most pleasant job!

If you want to avoid that work, if you want a clean crib, don't have any oxen. But without the oxen, you certainly won't get the work done! When we start doing something new or different, even in the Kingdom of God, we are going to have to clean out the proverbial barn.

Suppose you are singing a solo and you make a mistake. So what? The only people who don't make mistakes are the ones who never do anything. Their crib is always clean, but there are no oxen in the barn!

"*Yes, but* I'm a worm."

"Fear not, thou worm Jacob, and ye men of Israel; I will help thee, saith the Lord, and thy redeemer, the Holy One of Israel" (Isaiah 41:14).

That's what the Bible says. "Fear not, thou worm Jacob." But there is something more that I want you to see from that scripture. Now whenever the Bible mentions "the God of Jacob," we should be excited. Why? Who was Jacob? Jacob was a scheming, conniving, deceiving rascal that God changed into a saint. So every time the Bible mentions "the God of Jacob," it announces to us that we, with all our faults and deceptions, can become dynamic people of faith through the God of Israel.

"Fear not thou worm Jacob, deceiver. I specialize in making saints out of deceivers." We need to get loose of our billy-goat faith. Daniel 11:32 says, "The people that do know their God shall be strong, and do exploits."

"For all things are yours" (1 Corinthians 3:21).

"Ye are complete in Him, which is the head of all principality and power" (Colossians 2:10).

"In whom (Christ) are hid all the treasures of wisdom and knowledge" (Colossians 2:3).

Do you believe the Bible? Do you believe that all wisdom and knowledge is hid in Christ Jesus? Do you believe that Jesus is hid in you?

Then, *believe* that all the treasures of wisdom and knowledge are hid *in you.*

Once that faith is planted in your heart, begin to confess it! "I have the wisdom of God. I have the knowledge of God. God is going to show me how to do a better job of everything I do. God's know-how is in me. I don't know how to fail!"

We have more wisdom in us than could ever be found in any combination of Ph.D.'s. Jesus is in us! Right now!

"Yes, but I'm not saved."

"Say not in thine heart, Who shall ascend into heaven? (that is, to bring Christ down from above:)

Or, Who shall descend into the deep? (that is, to bring up Christ again from the dead.) But what saith it? The word is nigh thee, even in thy mouth, and in thy heart: that is, the word of faith, which we preach; That if thou shalt confess with thy mouth the Lord Jesus, and shalt believe in thine heart that God hath raised him from the dead, thou shalt be saved. For with the heart man believeth unto righteousness; and with the mouth confession is made unto salvation" (Romans 10:6-10).

Christ has already come. The Word doesn't say, "Who is *going* to raise Him from the dead?" Jesus has *already been raised* from the dead.

In other words, God has already done everything that needs to be done for your salvation. Christ has come. Christ has died. Christ has risen from the dead. Christ has ascended to the Father. Jesus has already died for your sins. He has already conquered the devil. Now all you need to do is confess it. Speak it out. The word of faith is near you. It's in your mouth, and in your heart.

What word? The word that Jesus is Lord and that He is alive and risen from the dead. Believe it and speak it. Confess it. Make a mouth confession of what you believe. Remember, if you speak it, you eat it; it becomes a part of you. Confess Jesus as your living Lord, and you will be saved. It will be the most important confession of your lifetime!

Chapter Five

Attempting to Manipulate God

The Bible says in Matthew 7:7-8, "Ask, and it shall be given to you; seek, and you shall find; knock, and it shall be opened to you. For every one who asks receives, and he who seeks finds, and to him who knocks it shall be opened" (*NAS*).

It says ask, seek, and knock. Many of us look at this type of scripture through our own particular pair of rose-colored glasses. These glasses, through which we like to read all promise scriptures, can often be greedy and full of self-interest. So through our rose-colored glasses we read:

Ask.....good job!

Seek.....new car!

Knock.....much money!

In our understanding of faith and mouth confession, we have to be careful not to try to manipulate God. Our sole concept of prayer should never be give me, give me, give me. We must learn God's balance between believing His Word and confessing it, or asking for many things based on our own self-interest. If we do get out of balance, and God doesn't come through in answer to our "give me" prayers, we become depressed, beligerent, or worst yet, disillusioned.

"How come, God? The Bible isn't true! The Bible says, 'Whatsoever things you desire, when you pray, believe that you have received them, and you will have them.' I have a lot of desires. How come you didn't answer me?"

We must be careful not to develop a "Jehovah is my servant" psychology, a "Get with it God" mentality. God is not our whim-satisfier, or fairy godmother. Remember those stories when you were a kid? The fairy godmother, in a white robe with a nice little gold sceptre, would sprinkle stardust and turn pumpkins into royal coaches. We must guard against having a fairy godmother view of prayer—new job, new car, much money.

Mouth confession should not be used as a magic wand. If our confessions are out of balance with the total Word and the whole council of God, our interpretation of Scripture can take on a greedy and grasping nature. "God, You rub my back, and I'll rub Your back. Now look, God, I am being obedient, and I'm witnessing, and I'm making the right confessions. Now surely You can come through for me." Then we get depressed when we don't get our way.

Let's look again at this promise of ask-seek-knock. The Scriptures say, "Ask and it's given, seek and you find, and knock and it's opened to you." To me, this scripture describes three levels of Christian growth and maturity. "First you *receive,* then you *find*, then it is *opened.*" There is a distinction. There is a place for the first level of *asking* and *receiving*. In fact, asking and receiving is a Christian faith builder—an encouragement to go on to more growth. The whole emphasis on asking is receiving. When we ask and receive, it confirms to us that God is faithful to His Word.

So, in the beginning, you ask and receive. But I believe that when people go on to *seek,* then they begin to *find*. Seekers find such things as that God doesn't want them sick. They begin to find that the baptism in the Holy Spirit is real, and they begin to seek to be full of the Holy Spirit. Seekers begin to find out about spiritual gifts. They find they don't have to live in sin. They find they don't have to have back trouble or migraine headaches. They find they don't have to go around lusting. They find they don't have to be unforgiving or bitter. (See my book, *Freedom To Choose*, for a full discussion of forgiveness.)

Seekers find far more than how to obtain forgiveness of sins. The new birth is the imperative first step to Christian growth. But seekers find many glorious victories as they grow in Jesus. They become successful and enthusiastic Christians. The seeker finds things in Christ that the asker does not even know are available.

Now we understand that the asker receives, and the seeker finds, but I believe it's the one who knocks who comes to know *who God really is.* The one who knocks presses on to know the very character and nature of God. There is a great deal of difference in *what God does* for you and *who God is.* I'll try to explain. Suppose a wife was only interested in her husband because of what he could do for her and what he would give her. What if the wife said, "I don't care who you are, I just want to know what you will give me." That's pretty ridiculous, isn't it? But do you see the distinction? When I married Dee, she knew what I did and what I believed, but she didn't really know who I was. But as we were married ten years, twenty-five years, and more, she now knows not only what I do, but who I am. I believe there are people in our congregation who also know who I am well enough that they can predict with ninety-five percent accuracy how I'd respond in a given situation.

I believe, in the same way, you can know who God is, how He thinks, how He reacts, what His character is. The character of God can be found throughout the Bible. If you make a study of Scripture for the express purpose of learning the character of God, you can come to know Him in such a way as to be able to predict what God will do in a given situation. It is immature and childish for us to want God to do something for us, *but not to want God.* Suppose a wife or a husband said to their spouse, "You want what I can do for you, but you don't want me. All you want is what I can give you." Well, I'm glad we can have health and joy and prosperity and answers to prayer from God, but what could be better than to be a friend of God? The Bible says that Abraham was called the friend of God.

Let's think for a bit about being a friend of God. I believe it can be opened up to you *who* God is, not just *what* God does. When I have friends in our home for an evening and it approaches eleven o'clock, they say "good night," and depart. We don't end our friendship, but we do become separated until we meet again. But with God, He never has to go home. He will always be present with us.

I have been practicing the presence of Jesus. It seems that I'm always busy with things, with people, with phone calls. So now, I just sit back for a bit. It doesn't take long. I tell my secretary, "Just put that person on hold for a minute." Then I sit back and just say, "Jesus, Jesus, Jesus. I really love You, Lord. You're so tender. You're so good to me." I just sit for a few moments and appreciate His presence. This is so different from yoga. We don't have an unknown mantra. We have a name: Jesus! Jesus! We have a name we can say over and over again: Jesus! Just whisper His name and you live in His presence: the very presence of God. Living in the presence of God is so much easier than having to continually overcome sin. I know it is! Who wants to be sin-conscious? You can be God conscious. God can be your perpetually present friend. Just practice living in the Spirit, and you will have victory.

I'm reminded of a woman who came to me for counseling. She was bitter, angry, and unforgiving.

She had previously been in a mental institution. I didn't say to her, "You need to get the hate out of you. You need to repent." I said, "Well, you know, Jesus said, 'I have come that you might have abundant life.' And you aren't experiencing the abundant life, and you're not happy. What would it take to make you happy? I want to see you happy. I want to see you smile." And I just began to listen to God and to just kind of flow with that person in the Spirit. I said, "You know you're never going to be happy as long as you're mad at everybody." She said, "I know that's right." "Well," I told her, "you ought to get rid of your anger." Within only ten minutes of loving that person and just flowing with the presence of God, she was praying and asking the blood to cleanse away all of her hate. She smiled, and I said, "Man, that's a neat smile." I just began to build her up and receive her as a person.

It's so neat to meditate on the presence of God and to live in the presence of God. We need to have a fellowship with God, a friendship with God. Now you know that you can't have friends if you don't talk *to them*. You can't be a friend of God, then if you don't talk to Him. That's prayer. It's also true that you can't have a friend when you don't give that person equal opportunity to talk *to you*. So, just as important as talking to God, is listening to what He is saying to you. Friendship goes both ways. Talk and listen. Now, it's very unusual to hear the audible voice of God, but just be quiet and expectantly listen for that still, small voice of the Lord. As you keep your mind stayed on Him, be alert for the thoughts and answers that God speaks to your spirit. That's the voice of God!

Let's stop everything right now and ask our Father, our best Friend, to speak to us. Just set your mind on Jesus. Open up! Wait!.... Did God speak to you? Do you know what He said to me? God said, "Just fellowship with Me." Now if we fellowship with God all the time, we'll never sin, will we? God wants our fellowship. He wants us to know Him, not just for what He'll do for us, not just for what He'll give us. He wants us, our fellowship, and our friendship.

It's a good thing God doesn't give us everything we desire and ask of Him in prayer. Have you noticed that your desires change when you abide in Christ? Jesus said, in Mark 11:24, "What things soever ye desire, when ye pray, believe that ye receive them, and ye shall have them." That scripture is true, but those things you desire change when you're right with God, when you're in the Spirit. I do not believe that God will answer your prayer for your desires to be fulfilled when you're out of the Spirit. I believe that the blanket promise of Mark 11:24 is conditional upon you being right with God.

"What things soever ye desire...." Let's take dating for example. If you're young and single and out of the Spirit, you might desire to date a certain blonde. You say, "Lord, I confess in the name of Jesus that that blonde will certainly date me." That might be the worst thing that ever happened to you.

So it's good that God doesn't answer all our prayers. You might end up married to the wrong woman, or the wrong man. God may have had a totally different plan for your life. The same thing applies to jobs, or to any other desire. Unless we are right with God, walking in the Spirit, fellowshipping with Him, asking and listening for His answer, we can easily be harmed by our desires. But when we are in fellowship with God, our desires change and come in line with God's desires for us. Would you be willing to pray, "God, if I ask for something dumb, that's going to hurt me, please cancel out my prayer, no matter how much faith I have"? Would you be afraid to pray that prayer?

Here's another thought. *Everything that you lift up higher than Jesus is an idol.* Even good things can be idols. Take a husband and wife for example. Proverbs 18:22 says, "He who finds a wife finds a good thing, and obtains favor from the Lord." But if you put your wife ahead of Jesus, she has become an idol. A husband is a good thing. Having a car is a good thing. A house for your family is a good thing. But if you lift any of these things higher than Jesus, it has become an idol. To many Christians, health is their idol. It becomes of primary importance to them. Why can't people be as excited about holiness and purity as they are about their new knowledge of nutrition? Good stewardship of our bodies is essential, but Jesus should always come first!

Search your life. Is there anything you are more concerned with than you are with Jesus? Cast down those idols!

Here's another statement. *Don't bother to claim the blanket promises of God if Jesus is not your Lord.* Look at these scriptures:

"The Lord is far from the wicked, but He hears the prayer of the righteous" (Proverbs 15:29). "He who turns away his ear from listening to the law, even his prayer is an abomination" (Proverbs 28:9). "If I regard wickedness in my heart, the Lord will not hear; But certainly God has heard; He has given heed to the voice of my prayer" (Psalm 66:18-19, *NAS*).

God is saying, "Hey, forget about making a list of your desires if you aren't right with Me. Your desires are so off-base and vested in self-interest that you're wasting your time." You see, we cannot manipulate God. He is the Creator; we are the created, the creature. We don't give the Creator orders. "Here's my list, God. Get with it." God says, "I'm not about to fill all your desires. You haven't repented. You're not right with Me. You're not seeking Me and My Kingdom first. I have other desires for you that would be better." The first and most important prayer is for repentance and forgiveness—getting right with God—getting our relationship with Jesus established. After that, our desires will more easily fall in line with His desire to bless us.

Proverbs 10:3 says, "The Lord will not allow the righteous to hunger, but *He will thrust aside the craving of the wicked*" *(NAS)*. So God says, "If you're in right standing with Me, you will have plenty of food. I promise it. But, if you're wicked, I'll thrust aside your cravings." That verse is crystal clear, isn't it? I'll guarantee you, people will try, but they'll never manipulate God. God is God. He is the Creator. We are His created. Remember, He's not a fairy godmother. We are very foolish if we think that the promises of asking, seeking and knocking mean only material and monetary gain. "Ask, and it shall be given" represents only the first level of getting to know God. "Seek, and you shall find," and we begin to find the power and the promises of God. Then, when we "knock, and it shall be opened unto you" we discover who God is, and we begin to know *Him,* instead of just what He can *give* us. We begin to love and to fellowship with Him. We begin to find out His ways and His character. Then He becomes a friend, and so personal to each of us that we can be aware of His living inside of us at all times: The revelation of "Christ in you, the hope of glory" (Colossians 1:27).

When you have a close relationship with God, He will give you the desires of your heart because His desires and your desires have become one. When the Holy Spirit is dropping the will of God into your heart, then, "what things soever you desire, when you pray...you shall have them." So faith and mouth confession have to remain in balance with knowing God and His desire for us.

God will not be manipulated. He's God. He's Sovereign. He will not be ruled by man. He will give us throne-rights, but He will never give us the throne.

But as we get to know Him through our Lord Jesus Christ, we can also be His friends, with the freedom to grow in His friendship and in His love.

Chapter Six

Goals For Living

When I graduated from high school and was called of God to preach, I established, with God's affirmation, a goal of preparation for the ministry which included four years of college and three years of seminary training. I had no financial help, and we had four children before I was out of college. Thus, it took me nine years to complete seven years of higher education. But—I had a goal; I knew where I was headed and why. I had established a goal, and I grew and matured as I sought to accomplish that goal.

In order to experience a fruitful and successful life, we each need to have specific directions for every area of our lives. We need family and marital goals, vocational and financial goals and, certainly, spiritual and fellowship goals. These goals will give us a path to follow in a world filled with diversions.

A real cause of frustration is that many people establish very vague goals for themselves. For example, suppose that you set a goal to have family devotions. You will also need to take certain steps to allow you to fully implement that goal. You will need to decide such things as, "What is the best time of day for our devotions?" "How can we proceed without that time becoming just another church service and turning the kids off?" "Does the Lord want us to do it?" You should prayerfully consider all of these questions. The Lord may lead you to establish your devotions immediately after the evening meal. You may be led to have just a short time of prayer and Scripture sharing. Whatever steps you take, you need to consider all such details.

Maybe you want to set a goal to lose thirty pounds. Merely setting the goal isn't enough. You will need to decide on specific steps, such as, "I will not eat desserts," or, "I'm not going to eat a bite between meals." Those decisions must be made.

Suppose your goal is to read through the Bible this year. You will never accomplish it unless you make up your mind to set aside a specific time each morning or evening to read the Scriptures. One of my children has read the Bible through each year for the past three years now. It can be done. But, perhaps you are the type of person who gets so blessed by reading Scripture that you can't seem to keep a specific reading schedule. Well, don't worry about it. If you get halfway through the Bible this year, then finish the second half next year. You are still receiving the benefits of reading more of the Bible than before. You see, your goal is not your god, but you are progressing toward its accomplishment.

It is very important that our goals never be

allowed to become gods or idols to us. Goals are intended to *serve us*. We are not meant to *serve our goals*. In other words, we should decide on our goals, but we may, after a year or so, change or alter our decisions. We must not be totally bound by them. The Lord Jesus Christ is our God. Our goals are not our god. So what if it takes you two years to finish the Bible instead of one? At least you are not just drifting along as a "status quo" person.

At every age and every stage of life, it is vital that we establish personal goals in order to avoid becoming "status quo" persons. These are people who either lack goals in their lives or make no plans to implement their goals. Not sure what they want out of life, they drift from one interest to another, and eventually become stagnant socially, emotionally and, most important, spiritually.

Drifting without plan or purpose is often excused with, "I want to, but I just can't find the time." I have three convictions about time. First, each of us has twenty-four hours every day. Second, you have time to do what you want to do. Third, we all tend to be crybabies about how busy we are. I know men and women who don't even work. Talk to them. They're too busy to find the time for a job. It's true. Even the laziest person thinks he or she is too busy. Personally, I refuse to accept this idea for myself. I choose to believe that I have time to do what I want to do. If you want to watch a professional ball game on T.V., or whatever, you'll find the time to do it! If you have permission from the Lord, then do it. You also have time to do more constructive things. It's just a question of doing what you choose to do.

Let's look at God's Word.

Proverbs 12:24, "The hand of the diligent will rule, but the slack hand will be put to forced labor."

Proverbs 12:27, "A slothful man does not roast his prey, but the precious possession of a man is diligence."

Proverbs 13:4, "The soul of the sluggard craves and gets nothing, but the soul of the diligent is made fat."

Proverbs 13:18, "Poverty and shame will come to him who neglects discipline, but he who regards reproof will be honored" (*NAS*).

I believe that one characteristic of a genuine Christian is good work habits. The fact that you are saved should show in your working to make your boss successful. We can preach about smoking, drinking, cussing, etc., but that can be misleading. Most of us don't practice those things. I believe that the evidence of a Christian should be in how he works, not primarily in whether he smokes. (However, I don't want you to smoke; I don't want you to get lung cancer!)

One Christian businessman told me, "I won't hire Christians. They backbite, nit-pick and are lazy. They think that because I'm a Christian boss, they don't have to work hard, and they can get away with anything. I hire non-Christians, then I lead them to the Lord, and they're okay." How sad! When I preached this from the pulpit, somebody shouted,

"That doesn't make sense." I replied, "Amen, it sure doesn't."

Picture people in the work force who don't smoke, but they don't get their work done either. You can't depend on them. They don't have any initiative. They won't go ahead on their own unless you mark out every step for them. You couldn't promote them. You couldn't put them in a position of responsibility. Frankly, I believe the boss would say, "I just wish they would work. I could care less about whether they smoke or not. I just wish they'd work." Somehow, Christians have got to understand that being a Christian means being the best employee the boss has ever seen. It means being on time, being diligent, doing the extra things, and doing everything possible to make the boss successful. Maybe from the pulpit we've overemphasized smoking and underemphasized working.

There is another aspect concerning laziness and its effect on you. I worked my way through college with a job at Boeing Aircraft. My immediate foreman came to me one day, saying, "Look, you're doing the work of two men in one shift. Stop it. You're working yourself out of a job." I've never forgotten that. I now understand why airplanes cost so much, but I don't accept that philosophy. I know that when I was busy and went home dead-tired, I felt good; but when we weren't busy and sat around for hours, I felt numb from boredom. Whether you're a production worker, an office worker, or a housewife, when you're busy and get a lot done, you have a sense of accomplishment. You feel great. But when you have nothing to do, it depresses you. Strange as it may seem, work is more fun than games. Do you believe that? It's a principle—even with your children. If you will go outside and work in the yard with your children, you'll actually have more fellowship and more fun than if you play Monopoly, particularly if you lose. No one loses when they work. But you can become depressed if you're too lazy to work and fulfill your responsibilities.

I am excited about the fact that God is the Creator. It says in Genesis that the waters of the earth teemed with swarms of living creatures. I can just visualize how the seas bubbled with life and how pleased and excited God was. I realize that we, being made in the image and likeness of God, need to be creative, full of energy, busy and excited about things other than just drifting along. I think we're half dead if we don't have goals. In all aspects, it's better to establish goals, even if we don't reach them, even if we have to alter them.

You may have a goal to get out of debt. Having the goal is of no value unless you also decide how much you will apply to the eradication of your debts, and schedule your payments. It may be that you will be led to tear up your credit cards. I'm not telling you to do that, but I am saying that you will need to take whatever steps are necessary to reach your goal.

Earlier, I mentioned that we need to set fellowship goals. Fellowship is very important in every Christian life. If you don't have friends in your church, it is only a matter of time until you will leave it. Regardless of whether you're a senior citizen, a young married couple, a college or a high school student, you must have friends. You could just sit around and moan about being lonely. But what's your goal for fellowship? If you are a young married couple you might establish steps to fulfill your fellowship goal by saying, in effect, "We will invite three couples to our home once each month." Whatever you can do, do it! Set your goal; pray about it; plan how to implement it; schedule it; do it!

One young, discouraged college girl came to me, saying, "I'm lonely. I don't have any friends." I said to her, "Do you know where all those college-age kids sit in church?" She said, "Yes." I replied, "Well, go over and plop yourself right down in the middle of them." She said, "But, I'm shy." "Well," I told her, "choose to get over it. Start showing yourself friendly. To have friends, you have to be a friend. Start talking to everyone in your age group. When we announce a canoe trip, you sign up. When we announce a ski trip, sign up; skating, go; volleyball, be there. Every activity, whatever it is, be there." You know, she did that and developed so much fellowship that she got married within a year! I have said the same thing to other young people who still just sit back with their one or two friends and complain about how lonely they are. Part of the responsibility for fellowship is on your church staff, but part of the responsibility is also yours. You need to set a fellowship goal, plan an approach, and then do it.

Marriage is an important goal. Unless God bestows the gift of celibacy upon someone, as He occasionally (but rarely) does, I believe that a normal young person would be thinking about marriage at some point once they finish school. I know I did. I wanted a wife and I wanted children. God said that it is not good for man (or woman for that matter) to dwell alone. And I agree with Him. But you can't just sit on your status quo and wish you were married. Again, you are going to have to take steps to fulfill your marriage goal, and some of those steps are described above in our discussion about fellowship goals. Be in prayer, be friendly, and be involved in the appropriate activities.

Now for some of us who are getting older, I want to repeat an earlier warning. Don't ever allow yourself to become a status quo person. I believe it is hazardous to your spiritual and mental health when you cannot accept your age. The Bible says that in whatever state you find yourself, you are to be content. At this writing, I am 47. When I turned 47, I was glad I was 47. I didn't want to be 50, and I didn't want to be 40. I did not "cross over the hill" at age 40. You need to enjoy every age of your life, and if you don't, you need to repent, because the word "repent" means "to change your mind." We should be glad when we're thirty, forty, or sixty. We can enjoy our children when they're babies, when they're toddlers, when they're in grade school, in high school, and when they are grown. All times should be equally enjoyable. Be content in whatever state you find yourself. I think you have a real mental problem if you're trying to be thirty when you're forty, or trying to be twenty when you're thirty. All I want is good health, at whatever age I am. I am enjoying my forties, just as I enjoyed my thirties. Be content, whatever your state.

"Not that I have already obtained it, or have already become perfect, but I press on in order that I may lay hold of that for which also I was laid hold of by Christ Jesus.

"Brethren, I do not regard myself as having laid hold of it yet; but one thing I do: forgetting what lies behind and reaching forward to what lies ahead,

"I press on toward the goal for the prize of the upward call of God in Christ Jesus" (Philippians 3:12-14, *NAS*).

In this scripture, Paul is first admitting that he isn't the kind of person, or the kind of Christian, he knows he should be. He says he has not yet obtained it. And neither have I obtained it. Paul admits, in verse 12, that he has not reached perfection, but that he presses on in order to lay hold of it. But, you say, "Can anyone ever expect to be perfect?" In Philippians 1:6 Paul says, "For I am confident of this very thing, that He who began a good work in you will perfect it until the day of Christ Jesus" (*NAS*). So you see, perfection is not beyond reaching for. Mentally, it's a healthy thing to recognize and admit that you haven't arrived yet; haven't obtained your goal.

Satan would like to have you think that the preacher has arrived. You say, "Oh, if I could just be like the pastor, or that Sunday School teacher, or that elder." But we haven't arrived! Just think, Paul was one of the greatest Christians who ever lived. Yet he said, "I haven't obtained it, and I'm not perfect." It's healthy to admit that neither you, nor anyone else, is where they want to be spiritually. It's a delusion to believe you've arrived, and it's good to admit you haven't. I don't know of anyone who is satisfied with the kind of dad or mom or child that they are now. The devil wants you to be under condemnation and discouragement. So you haven't arrived! So join the human race! So you haven't obtained it! Neither have I! You see, the first thing is, *admit it.*

The second thing Paul says is, "forgetting all things that are past." I have always loved this verse because he says, "but one thing I do...," and you might think he's going to be super-spiritual and say, "but one thing I do, I just worship the Lord," or "but one thing I do, I read the Scriptures every day." But what is it that Paul says he does? He says, "One thing I do...forget what lies behind..." That's true wisdom! You have to forget yesterday's victories. You can't live on yesterday's spirituality!

You must also forget yesterday's defeats; those all lie behind. They're over with, water under the bridge. You can't go back to them. Put them under the blood of Jesus and get up and go on! *Admitting* and *forgetting* are both mental and spiritual necessities.

The third thing Paul says in the passage is, "and

reaching forward to what lies ahead, I press on toward the goal...." He says, "I reach forward," and he says, "I press on." I believe that many people are willing to admit that they are not what they ought to be. Many also believe that the blood of Jesus has cleansed them, so they are not under condemnation. But—they've stopped reaching. Unless you are also reaching, I tell you, you are likely to become discouraged or depressed. You should never allow yourself to become a status quo person and say, "I'll get up, go to work, come home, go to bed, go to church twice a week, and I guess that's life." No wonder you're depressed. You need to have goals. And then you need to reach forward toward them.

Do what needs to be done. Don't settle down where you are. Don't pitch your tent and say, "Well, this is where I am, and this is where I'll park it." You have to have some activity, some interest, something ahead that you are reaching toward. In fact, if you don't have the following three principles at work in your life, you will be out of balance spiritually and mentally. You have to *admit* realistically that you have some growing yet to do. You have to *forget* the mistakes you've made, and even the victories you've experienced. You also have to continue to *reach* for something better. You have to set goals and grow into them.

Chapter Seven

Principles That Work

Through the years I have heard many people say, "I tried Christianity, but it didn't work for me. It may be your bag, but I tried Christ and it didn't last. I prayed and I prayed, but nothing happened. God failed me."

Why do people talk like that? How can it be so?

First, *God always works on the basis of principles*, not on the basis of magic. If you don't understand that, then you are going to be confused about Christianity. God always works on the basis of principles.

One of God's principles is demonstrated in the following scripture: "Do not be deceived, God is not mocked; for whatever a man sows, this he will also reap. For the one who sows to his own flesh shall from the flesh reap corruption, but the one who sows to the Spirit shall from the Spirit reap eternal life" (Galatians 6:7-8, *NAS*).

Whatever it is that we plant, that is what we will reap. If you sow fleshly things, the Word says you will reap corruption. If, however, you sow spiritual things, you will reap eternal life.

Do you have enough faith to believe that if you went out to the back yard and prayed over the ground, without plowing and without planting, saying, "In the name of Jesus I ask for a beautiful, bountiful garden," that suddenly a row of carrots would pop up, and then a row of beans and a row of corn? I know that all things are possible with God, but do you have enough faith to believe for a garden without planting a garden? Friends, it just won't happen that way. And yet, in the spiritual realm, people very often expect that type of instantaneous happening. Spiritually, they think they can plant just one seed a week, and pray when they get into trouble. Or they might decide to read the Bible maybe twice a month; that's two seeds. They plant two or three seeds a month, and then they look to their spiritual garden and say, "God, you failed me! Where are the results? Where are the vegetables? I prayed and You didn't come through! It didn't work for me."

There is a joke about a preacher who went to visit one of his parishioners and found him out in the back yard in his garden. The preacher looked at the beautiful garden, every row straight, full of every kind of vegetable. There were beans and peas and cauliflower and lettuce and carrots. "Boy," he said, "you and the Lord sure have a beautiful garden." And the old boy leaned on his hoe and replied, "Yes, but you should have seen it when the Lord had it all by Himself."

You know, I don't think that joke offends God at all. I think that joke has a great deal of spiritual truth in it. It illustrates one of God's principles: you are going to get exactly what you plant, no more, and no less. We cannot make God the scapegoat for our lack of planting seeds!

Let's examine this principle in even more detail. Take, for instance, a family that understands the principles of raising children. They may be ignorant of the Bible, but they know about discipline and they know about love. So, mom and dad follow those two principles. They may not know that they are Biblical principles, but, in practice, they balance love with discipline. That home has structure and authority. The parents don't allow the children to do just anything they want, but yet the children know they are loved and they know the boundaries of discipline. Even though the parents are non-Christians, because they follow Biblical principles, those children are going to become well-balanced young adults. God operates on the basis of principles.

In contrast, consider another family. They go to church every Sunday, yet they are harsh and mean to their children about some things. Then they allow them to do pretty much as they want the rest of the time. When the child reaches the age of sixteen, his parents buy him a car, and from then on, they seldom see that teenager. That child is going to end up a rascal, and God is going to be blamed for it! But the parents didn't understand that God operates on the basis of principles.

It is not some magical thing. You can't just do your own thing, follow your own will, be rebellious, and then push a God-button and say, "Okay, God, please cause my children to be holy." God just cries when he hears that. If you would listen to Him, He would say, "Can't you see that you are violating every scripture in My book? You're setting a poor example for them. You're teaching them wrong attitudes. You're closer to the devil's side than you are to Mine. There is strife, swearing, fighting, and unreasonableness. Then you dare to think that by praying one prayer your family will turn out fine. You're living the devil's way day and night. How can I . . . ?"

Then they will say, "Well, I don't know. I prayed for my kids. I don't know what happened. I prayed and God didn't answer my prayer. I tried Christianity, but it didn't work for me."

God will answer prayer, but there must be reality about it, such as, "God, help me to start keeping my mouth shut." "God, help me not to pick on my children and let me be more reasonable." Prayers have to be based on some *reality!* Remember, God operates on the basis of principles, not magic.

God has many principles. Here's another one: "Be ye not unequally yoked together with unbelievers." One clear application of that verse is: Don't marry a non-Christian. Yet, how many Christians have married non-Christians, and then experienced years of heartache and sorrow? And guess who gets the blame for it? They blame God. They disobeyed the Word of God, they violated God's principle, then they blame Him for the results. We reap what we sow.

Another principle that always works: we will get out of our walk with Christ what we put into it. Read 2 Corinthians 9:6-8, "Now this I say, he who sows sparingly shall also reap sparingly; and he who sows bountifully shall also reap bountifully. Let each one do just as he has purposed in his heart; not grudgingly or under compulsion; for God loves a cheerful giver. And God is able to make all grace abound to you, that always having all sufficiency in everything, you may have an abundance for every good deed" (*NAS*).

The Scriptures say, if you sow sparingly you will reap sparingly. You see, there are financial principles in the Kingdom of God. If we violate those financial principles, we suffer accordingly. I get just a little upset about people violating every scripture and then wondering what went wrong with their lives. Then they have the audacity to blame God for their problems. You must understand that God always operates on the basis of His Word, on what the Word says. In Jeremiah 1:12 God says, "I am watching over My word to perform it." When you do what the Word says, you will get what the Word says. Praying a quickie prayer and violating every scripture is not going to produce a garden of holiness, happiness and well-being in your life or in your family.

If you sincerely want to learn about God's principles without studying the whole Bible, then just do a "cause-effect" study of thirty-one chapters of the Bible. Begin to carefully read the book of Proverbs. As you read, just write in a C (for cause) or an E (for effect) beside every appropriate verse. You'll find that you have either a C or an E beside nearly 80% of the verses in Proverbs.

Now, to whet your appetite, get your Bible out and let's look at Proverbs 28, verse 27, which reads, "He who gives to the poor will never want, but he who shuts his eyes will have many curses"(*NAS*). Now, whether you believe the Bible or not, God is going to operate by that verse. Whether you're a Christian or a non-Christian, if you open your eyes to the poor, and say, "Here is a family who needs groceries," or, "Here's someone who needs help with their utility bill," and then help them, God says you will never want. But, He says, if you shut your eyes to the needs of the poor, you'll have many curses come upon you. You may not have known that that verse was in the Bible until right now, but you are receiving in accordance with that verse and so am I.

Look at Proverbs 28:9, "He who turns away his ear from listening to the law, even his prayer is an abomination" (*NAS*). The *cause*, failing to listen to the law, brings the *effect*, unanswered prayer. When someone says, "God doesn't answer my prayers," the Bible says that if you turn your ear away from paying attention to the law or to the Word of God, then God will count your prayers as an abomination. So repentance must proceed God's moving on our behalf.

Proverbs 24:24 and 25 reads, "He who says to the wicked, 'You are righteous,' peoples will curse him, nations will abhor him; but to those who rebuke the wicked will be delight, and a good blessing will come upon them" (*NAS*).

Did you know that was in the Bible? The Bible says that if you reverse moral values; if you say to wicked people that they are righteous; if you see someone living in adultery and you say, "Oh well, that's all right, they love Jesus," then the Bible says that people will curse you and nations will abhor you. However, the Bible says that if you rebuke that person, saying, "What you are doing is sin, plain and simple," a blessing will come upon you. When you reverse moral values, you get into trouble, but when you take a stand for righteousness, God says He will bless you.

Here's another principle with a cause and effect. Turn to Proverbs 20:20, "He who curses his father or his mother, his lamp will go out in time of darkness" (*NAS*). Or, Proverbs 20:7, "A righteous man who walks in his integrity; how blessed are his sons after him"—another spiritual principle. This same principle is repeated in Ephesians 6:2-3 in the New Testament. The principle is that if you honor and obey your father and mother, things will go well for you. During counseling sessions, I have asked young people who have been involved with drugs and other sin, "Has it been going well with you?" These youngsters have been in rebellion against their homes. Every one of them have said, "It has not gone well. It's been very, very bad."

You must thoroughly understand that God works on the basis of principles. Some people want a "God-button." In other words, they want to do whatever pleases them. They violate every scripture in the Bible. They go against the laws of God and the laws of man. They reap all kinds of trouble and heartache. Then they think they can just push a God-button about once a week and get God to move on their behalf.

Sorry, it just doesn't work that way. "God is not mocked. Whatever a man sows, this will he also reap." Don't be just a two or a three or a four seed planter. Plant kindness. Plant God's love. Plant faith. Plant an appointment with God. Plant witnessing to others. Plant seeds in everything you do. God promises that you will reap bountifully. You will be happy. You'll have a good marriage. You will be successful. Your kids will turn out right. Why? Because you are living by the principles of God.

Many people also need to be jolted awake to the reality that we are locked into an intense spiritual warfare, that we have an adversary called the devil. The Bible, in Ephesians, speaks of principalities, powers, rulers and spirits doing continuous battle for your soul. One victory doesn't mean the battle is over or the war is won. Those principalities, powers, rulers, and spirits are arranged in an hierarchy of demonic forces that are real, that have pitted themselves against us. In their master plan, they have designed depression, despair, divorce, adultery, dishonesty, hatred, unforgiveness, and the breaking of every commandment of God. Those demonic spirits are pitted against us to press us down, to wipe out our marriages, our children and our very lives. It's a battlefield, brothers and sisters, not a picnic ground. We're going to have to be *awake and aware* of the reality that demons are working night and day to wipe us out.

"Be of sober spirit, be on the alert. Your adversary, the devil, prowls about like a roaring lion, seeking someone to devour. But resist him, firm in your faith, knowing that the same experiences of suffering are being accomplished by your brethren who are in the world. And after you have suffered for a little, the God of all grace, who called you to His eternal glory in Christ, will Himself perfect, confirm, strengthen and establish you. To Him be dominion forever and ever. Amen" (1 Peter 5:8-11, *NAS*).

The Bible says that the devil prowls about like a roaring lion, seeking someone to devour. Unfortunately, many Christians are asleep, apathetic and lukewarm. They don't even realize that they are in a spiritual battlefield, that life itself is a part of that battle. It's warfare. You have a supernatural enemy, and that enemy has a devious plan to wipe out your entire family. If you go to sleep at the wheel, and forget about the enemy, it can spiritually hurt or even kill you! You will find yourself away from the church and out of your walk with God. You may wake up a year later and find your marriage in trouble and your kids rebellious.

I know many people who had really become close to Jesus. They had prayed through and confessed all their sin. They felt the burden leave, and they were clean, pure, holy and excited about Jesus Christ. Now that's victory. But, as neat as it is at the time, a victory is different from a way of life. A lot of people assume that one victory means the end of the war. But, regardless of where we are in the Lord today, regardless of how much victory we have achieved, regardless of how much joy we have experienced, that does not yet mark the end of the war.

Remember what Paul said to Timothy as Paul's life was drawing to a close, "I have fought a good fight, I have finished my course, I have kept the faith" (2 Timothy 4:7). Paul was fully aware of the fight of faith we have as Christians. You might just as well make up your mind that you are going to stay in the Word and walk with the Lord; you're going to fight the battle through; and you're going to have more than just one victory—you're going to win the war! We are more than conquerors through Christ who loves us! (See Romans 8:37.)

One of God's ways of victory is worship. When you begin to learn how to worship God, then you will see Him move in your life. It's at that time, however, that Satan will try to come and steal your newfound freedom of worship away from you.

"Oh, I'm not going to lift my hands, or clap my hands in church. That's a bunch of nonsense."

But one of the secrets of God is that when you lift

your hands and begin to sing and worship Him, the Holy Spirit will anoint you, refresh you, move upon you, and get you back into victory, joy and peace.

It upsets me when I look out over a congregation and see people who won't worship. I'm upset knowing that Satan has deceived them and that it's because of him that they won't worship. They look down at their feet. They cross their arms. They look bored, because Satan has stolen their praise and their joy and their worship of God.

Look at 2 Corinthians 10:3-5, "Though we walk in the flesh, we do not war after the flesh: (for the weapons of our warfare are not carnal, but mighty through God to the pulling down of strongholds;) Casting down imaginations, and every high thing that exalteth itself against the knowledge of God, and bringing into captivity every thought to the obedience of Christ."

This scripture says that we are in a state of warfare. It says that we should be pulling down strongholds of Satan. Has Satan established some strongholds in you that need to be pulled down? You may have a stronghold of hate in your heart, and you need to say, "In the name of Jesus I am pulling that hate out of me. I am pulling down that Satanic stronghold." It's like the devil has a fortress in the corner of your heart, and you're going to have to release it and ask God to pull it out and tear it down.

Do you hate your mother-in-law? Is there a child that you resent? Are you bitter toward your spouse, or one of your parents? Through Christ we can forgive them and pull out that Satanic stronghold. It will bring peace of mind and health to your body.

Maybe you are bothered with unclean demonic spirits, sexual fantasies and such. The Scriptures say "casting down imaginations." We have the power in Jesus to cast down those thoughts, fantasies, "images" in our minds and bring into captivity every thought to the obedience of Christ.

"Cast down every high thing that exalts itself against the knowledge of God." Anything that destroys the knowledge of God in us—that draws us away from Christ Jesus—has got to be cast down or we will become lukewarm and apathetic. Brothers and sisters, we are in a warfare!

I believe two of the reasons why people say, "Well, it didn't work for me," are, first, they don't understand that God operates on the basis of principles. Second, they don't understand that there is an intense supernatural warfare led by a supernatural devil who is trying to wipe them out. It's a battlefield!

A third reason people become deceived and disillusioned about the Christian life is because they don't understand the vital importance of faith.

Hebrews 11:6 says, "Without faith it is impossible to please Him: for he that cometh to God must believe that He is, and that He is a rewarder of them that diligently seek Him."

Without faith it is not possible to please God: *that means that with faith you please God.*

Would you like to please God? What kind of faith

does it take? First, the Scriptures say that you must believe that God is—that God really exists.

Many times people who get into adultery and moral impurity stop believing that God is. As it says in Romans 1:28, "just as they did not see fit to acknowledge God any longer," because they know they are sinning against Him. An athiest is usually an athiest because he is into moral impurity or some other form of sin, and is trying to get rid of his guilt by throwing away his knowledge of God. If there isn't any God, then there isn't any guilt. If there isn't any God, then there isn't any judgment. Therefore, it's a very convenient way to avoid the need to repent. But, Scripture says that you must believe that God is.

Next, to have faith you must believe that God is a rewarder of them that diligently seek Him. Notice the word diligently! Are you really seeking God diligently? Are you having an appointment with God daily? Then God has promised to reward you.

Look more at this eleventh chapter of Hebrews. "Noah, by faith, being warned of God, *moved*...." He did something. Abel, by faith, *offered* a more excellent sacrifice. He did something. Abraham, by faith, *left* father, home, and nation and went to a strange country. He did something.

With faith, there is always action. Faith isn't passive. Faith doesn't sit back and say, "Yeah, I believe God exists." That passive belief is not what the Bible is talking about. Real faith is an active belief that God does reward those who diligently seek Him. So get with it. Have that special daily appointment with God. Get yourself to church on Sundays. Find a small group. Start studying the Scriptures, not with the idea of gaining head knowledge, but with the idea of "Lord, I will obey every word I read." If you are still walking in spiritual darkness, if you're still in willful sin and you pick up the Bible, I'll guarantee you that it will be a dead book. But when your heart is right, and you have confessed every sin you are aware of, and you open your Bible, you can say, "Lord, I don't want to just *read* Your Word, I want to *do* Your Word." When you are willing to obey God's Word, then He will cause you to understand His Word. I assure you that you will say, "God rewards everyone who diligently seeks Him."

Now, if you don't believe that, the Bible says it is impossible for you to please God. You are without faith. The reason you don't believe is probably because of unconfessed sin in your life which is blocking the flow and the power of God. Yes, God does reward those who diligently seek Him. I have seen it happen time and time again. I have experienced times when I have started to become lukewarm and have quit diligently seeking God. Then I see the anointing begin to wane and the blessings of God begin to dissipate. Quickly I get back into the Word and get with it in high gear, and God begins to bless and anoint again. He stands by His Word to perform it (Jeremiah 1:12).

You know, when you're right with God, there are just so many people to witness to, and you exude an excitement about Jesus. You receive the reward for your diligence now, not just after you die. He begins to reward you right there, that very day. There are, of course, rewards later, too, but you don't have to wait to be rewarded. He rewards those who diligently seek Him.

Yes, the Bible is true. Yes, the Bible is practical. Yes, the Christian life will work for you if you'll understand these things:

1. God operates on the basis of principles, not magic.

2. We are, and will continue to be, in an intense spiritual battle.

3. God is faithful to reward those who diligently seek Him.

Chapter Eight

Passing Life's Tests

"James, a bondservant of God and of the Lord Jesus Christ, to the twelve tribes who are dispersed abroad, greetings. Consider it all joy, my brethren, when you encounter various trials, knowing that the testing of your faith produces endurance. And let endurance have its perfect result, that you may be perfect and complete, lacking in nothing" (James 1:1-4, *NAS*).

How would you like to be complete, lacking in nothing? If you are like me, you would rather skip over verses two and three, and begin with verse four. But verses two and three tell us how to get to verse four. The testing and endurance, the trials, all have their perfect result, which is for us to be perfect and complete, lacking in nothing. James says we are to consider it all joy; in fact, the New International Version translates verse two, "pure joy." Can you consider life's trials and temptations pure joy? That's hard for me to do, and I would venture to say it is hard for most of you who are reading this to consider your trials and temptations pure joy—absolutely pure joy and nothing else mixed with it.

"I don't believe in trials," some Christians say.

"I don't believe God tests people," other Christians say.

But God says, "Consider it all joy, pure joy ...when you encounter various trials."

The Greek word here is *peiradzo,* which can be translated in either a bad sense or a good sense. *Peiradzo* in the good sense means "tests" or "to prove something." In the bad sense, it means "temptation" or "a trial."

You can trace this word throughout the New Testament, but in order to know how to translate it, you must know the context. The word "peiradzo" is found in each of the following scriptures regarding temptation.

"Lead us not into *temptation*" (Matthew 6:13).

"No *temptation* has overtaken you but such as is common to man; and God is faithful, who will not allow you to be *tempted* beyond what you are able, but with the *temptation* will provide the way of escape also, that you may be able to endure it" (1 Corinthians 10:13, *NAS*).

"Because you have kept the word of My perseverance, I also will keep you from the hour of *testing,* that hour which is about to come upon the whole world, to *test* those who dwell upon the earth" (Revelation 3:10, *NAS*).

Then, James says, "Consider it all pure joy when you encounter various *peiradzo.*" The Lord revealed to me one day that every temptation is always a test and every test is always a temptation. Both elements exist in every situation.

When I was in Africa on a teaching mission, I started teaching on this subject of tests and temptations, and the Lord said, "This didn't really get into your spirit. You taught it, but your church completely forgot it. Furthermore, you forgot it, too. When you get back, I want you to go over that again." So I sat down and studied it, and prayed about it, and thought about it some more. The following is what the Lord revealed to me and what I want to share with you.

In every instance in your life, every circumstance—indeed, every hour of every minute, every single day of your life—you are being faced with a situation that can be considered a test or a temptation. Satan is at work and God is at work in every facet of your life. From the devil's point of view, every situation is a *temptation,* but from God's point of view, it's a *test*. The devil has a purpose; to steal, to kill and destroy (John 10:10). Jesus has a purpose: that you be perfect, complete, lacking nothing (James 1:4). It's as simple as that.

Regardless of who *originated* an event or a circumstance, there are always three persons involved: God, the devil, and you. There are three wills involved: God's will, the devil's will, and your will. In every situation, there is interaction among these three purposes, these three wills.

For example, when the church I pastor, Full Faith

Church of Love in Kansas City, came into existence, obviously *God originated* that circumstance. The idea, the impetus and the help came from Him, and the church was dedicated to Him. But does that mean the devil isn't around this church? From the very beginning, he would have loved to infest Full Faith Church of Love with false doctrine, immorality, division and strife. Even though God started Full Faith, Satan is at work, watching for his chance, and we, the membership, can determine what is going to happen by which way we lean. Below is a drawing to illustrate this concept.

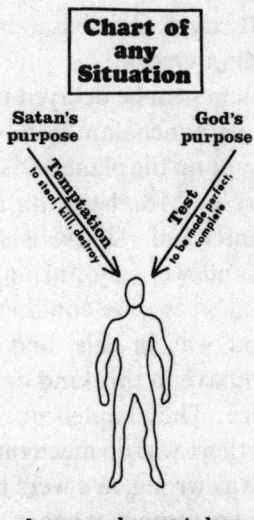

Chart of any Situation

Satan's purpose — Temptation: to steal, kill, destroy

God's purpose — Test: to be made perfect, complete

A person chooses to lean either to God's purpose or Satan's purpose.

In your own life, as in our church, God is always at work, Satan is always at work, and you are always at work.

Now, let's take a negative situation. In Africa, as our ministry group drove from western Kenya to Nairobi in the south-central area, the eight-hour trip over Kenya's antiquated roads was an experience in itself. There were two lanes, little or no shoulder, and our driver had a heavy foot. He liked to drive 70 miles an hour, swooping up, down, and around mountain curves as if he were taking us for a ride on the highest roller coaster ever built. After careening along all day, we arrived in Nairobi—exhausted, but thankful to be alive—only to sit around waiting for the airplane to fly us to Mombasa, on the southeast coast by the Indian Ocean.

"Well, your plane will be delayed two hours," the authorities told us nonchalantly. So we waited for two hours, then got on the plane and took off. When we were halfway to Mombasa, an announcement came over the intercom, "There is some difficulty with the plane, and we are returning to Nairobi." Being human and weary, we couldn't help wondering whether God was in this, and what possible reason He could have in this kind of difficulty. But we had no choice. They landed our plane back in Nairobi because there was no mechanic in Mombasa to fix whatever was wrong. We were herded into the deserted, dimly-lit airport where, exhausted, we spent two interminable hours trying to relax on the uncomfortable seats.

By this time, it was midnight, and we were all zombies. Frankly, my gall bladder was acting up, and I was feeling miserable. I tried to put up a good front, but Bud Sickler, our host and a missionary veteran of 35 years, guessed the truth. He sought out the captain in charge of the airplane and asked, "Could you let this man board the plane with his wife and be seated?"

The captain agreed, so my wife, Dee, and I trudged through the muggy darkness to the plane where I stretched out on two or three seats and went to sleep. This much-needed rest was God's relief for me, but He had used Bud to make it happen.

Here was a situation in a real, everyday life. Who was at work? Who caused that plane to be four or five hours late so that we found ourselves huddled in an unfamiliar, foreign airport in the middle of the night? Was it the devil? Was it God, asleep on the job of protecting our journey? Was it simply human error, some mechanic's carelessness?

Then, while I slept peacefully on the plane, where was Bud Sickler, who also had had a long drive that day and who was just as tired as my wife and me? He was left waiting in the airport. How did he respond to the situation? If he had leaned one way, in the direction of Satan's will, he would have been angry, out of the Spirit. It would have been a natural thing for him to lash out at the airplane personnel, for he was worn out. Instead, he leaned God's way and used the circumstance for the good.

There, in the Nairobi airport in the late hours of

the night, he met a young man, the son of a preacher. This fellow was either backslidden or had possibly never been saved. Bud Sickler began to talk with him, and soon he was pouring his heart out. He told Bud, "I've been condemned by all the Christians I know, but no one will answer my questions." For two hours, while Bud waited for the plane to be fixed, he talked to the young man about his soul and his salvation. Bud was able to bring this discouraged young person to a place of understanding that God loved him.

In this situation, if Bud had been out of the Spirit and resentful about losing his night's sleep in that hot, dusty airport in Nairobi, he could have lost the opportunity. If he had yielded to the *peiradzo,* the temptation, and lost his temper, he would have had no testimony for that young man. Because he responded correctly, he passed the *peiradzo,* the test, and had a marvelous opportunity to share his faith.

James 1:12 tells us, "Blessed is the man who perseveres under trial; for once he has been approved (or passed the test, as the margin says in the New American Standard Version), he will receive a crown of life which the Lord has promised to those who love Him." Remember, the Greek word *peiradzo* can be translated "temptation" or "test" and it should always be translated as both, because the devil wants every circumstance to be a temptation but God wants it to be a test. So if we persevere under trial, the Bible promises we'll be crowned with life. This doesn't mean that when we die we'll each get a crown that reads L-I-F-E in shining letters made of gold. It means we are crowned with life here and now.

That night in Nairobi, Bud Sickler was so happy to have the opportunity to talk to the troubled young man that he had no thought of fatigue or resentment. He passed the test. He was crowned with life.

Let me give you another illustration. I was at home waiting to use our family car. I needed to be at a wedding rehearsal a half hour's drive away, and my son brought the car home later than the time I had told him I'd need it. I didn't reprimand him, but just rushed outside, jerked open the car door and stuck the key into the ignition. I turned the key. The engine started but the gas gauge said, "E," and in this case E didn't stand for Ernie. There was enough gas left to get me to the corner filling station, which was very busy because it had the lowest price around. After I got in line, the man in front of me decided to check the air in his tires. He didn't even want gas! He just took his time and strolled around his automobile, carefully examining all four tires while I tried not to notice how the seconds and minutes were racing away on my watch.

By this time, a car had pulled up behind me and I was blocked in. I waited and waited while cars in line for the other pump came and went. This was irritating and made matters worse because I don't like to wait in line. At the discount house or the supermarket, I seem to have a special talent for landing in the slow line behind the man who is trying to write a check without having any ID or the woman who is waiting for the cashier to have someone find out the price of a blouse that doesn't have a tag.

Here I was at the filling station, waiting while the man ahead checked his tires, and by this time the smoke was coming out of my ears. Then, I realized I could lean either way. What the devil wanted me to do was go home that night and reproach my son, "You dumb kid, you're inconsiderate. You brought the car home late; you let it run out of gas." On the other hand, God wanted me to manifest His patience and joy. It was both a test and a trial!

The Lord told me, "You know what? You're always hurrying here and there and busy, busy, busy. I'm trying to work some patience into you." As it turned out, some members of the wedding party were late also, so my having been delayed caused no problem. I went home and didn't say a thing to my son about the car. Then I found out that, through no fault of his own, he'd had to search everywhere for some parts for his own car. He had driven across the entire metropolitan area, approximately 25 miles, to look for them. When he came home, he was discouraged because the parts weren't available. He'd had a bad day. There had been no sin on his part, no selfishness. Because I didn't chew him out, he could see Jesus in me. I passed the test, and I was crowned with life.

Of course, there have been many times when I didn't pass the test—times when, with my will, I leaned the other way and let the test become temptation. Then, something in a relationship was hurt, some joy was killed and somebody's spirit was wounded, just because I forgot to "count it pure joy."

Do you believe the Bible is true when in says, in Romans 8:28, "...we know that all things work together for good to them that love God, to them who are called according to His purpose"? Often, we misquote that verse. We leave out the first phrase, "we know," and most people quote it, but they don't know it. Or we leave out the last phrase, "to them who are called according to His purpose," and His purpose in each of our lives is usually different from our own purpose.

Do you believe in the sovereignty of God? If you believe what you are reading in this chapter, you'll never be in a bad mood. When something goes wrong, you'll say, "Wow! The Bible says count it pure joy! Hallelujah! Glory to God!" It isn't so much what happens, but how you respond to what happens, that counts.

One day in 1977, to my amazement, I passed pure blood in my urine. By the next morning, I was flip-flopping in excruciating pain on my bed. I was passing blood clots. I was taken to the hospital by the paramedics and within 48 hours the doctors found a cancer the size of my fist encapsulated in my right kidney. Now, where did that cancer come from? Who originated it? The devil did, but God wanted to deal with me, challenge me and cause me to seek His face. I was in the middle (see diagram on page 93) and in the case of cancer—sickness—Satan was the obvious originator. But God was at work also. He worked His way within my spirit as I successfully overcame the cancer with no reoccurance. (I had an operation for the removal of my right kidney.) Through it all, God gave me perfect peace and insisted on His absolute Lordship in my life.

"I'm confused," you may say. "Should I praise God or rebuke the devil." *Always do both.* The devil is in every situation; he must be stood against and rebuked. Likewise, God is in every situation; He must be sought and praised.

Regardless of who originates things, God is at work in every situation and Satan is at work in every situation. Sometimes God originates things, sometimes Satan originates things, and sometimes we originate things. What if you continuously overeat until you carry 50 to 100 more pounds than you should? Then you say, "Well, the devil gave me this physical problem." Who originated that overweight—you or the devil? Sometimes we are our own originators. Let's say you don't get adequate sleep; it will cause psychological manifestations. The psychologists teach that a person who doesn't get enough sleep for a period of three or four days will hallucinate. So, if someone doesn't get enough rest, doesn't eat the right kind of food, smokes pot, or whatever, his or her body responds by breaking down in one way or another. That person is the originator of his own poor health. If you have such a problem, I am sure Satan is involved as tempter, but still, your own will is involved as originator.

The diagram on page 93 applies to every instant of your life. In every moment, every phone call, every purchase in a store, every work day, every relationship—God has a purpose and Satan has a purpose, and you are in between. Your faith is being tested to see whether you will count all things pure joy. Faith produces endurance so that you don't give up. Let endurance have its perfect work, making you perfect and complete, lacking nothing. Blessed is the man or woman who passes the test, for that person had been approved. He or she is crowned with life.

Some people say God doesn't test us. How mistaken they are! God has been testing individuals since the earliest Old Testament times. He tested Abraham, the Israelites, and He tested His chosen leader, Moses. "Then the Lord said to Moses, 'Behold, I will rain bread from heaven for you; and the people shall go out and gather a day's portion every day, that I may *test* them, whether or not they will walk in My instruction'" (Exodus 16:4, *NAS*). "God has come in order to *test* you" (Exodus 20:20). "All the commandments that I am commanding you today you shall be careful to do, that you may live and multiply, and go in and possess the land which the Lord swore to give your forefathers. And you shall remember all the way which the Lord God has led you in the wilderness these forty years, that He might humble you, *testing* you..." (Deuteronomy 8:1-2, *NAS*).

God's purpose was for Moses to deliver His people, but Moses had a problem: Israel's stubbornness and Pharoah's stubbornness. Remember, the Israelites were not too happy to have Moses for a leader. And even before becoming their leader, he'd already had one serious problem. He had murdered an Egyptian, and as a result had spent 40 years in the wilderness. But he overcame and came into possession of God's purpose for his life. He led the children of Israel out of Egypt and to the gates of the promised land.

Sometimes God uses nations or individuals other than His own people to test us. In Judges, the nations of the five lords of the Philistines "were for *testing* Israel, to find out if they would obey the commandments of the Lord" (Judges 3:4). Perhaps Russia is testing the United States. Do not think this is impossible. You might say, "Yes, but they are a godless nation." God has used godless nations in the past to test nations that were more righteous.

The Scriptures are filled with examples of God's testing. Genesis 22 tells the story of how Abraham obeyed God's command and offered Isaac as a test of his obedience and how, at the last moment, God provided a sacrificial lamb in substitution for Isaac. The whole book of Job is the story of Job's testing. Some people may say, "But that's the Old Testament," as if the God of the Old Testament somehow switched His character when the New Testament was written. But Malachi 3:6 says with a firmness that rings to us across the ages, *"I the Lord do not change.* Therefore you, oh sons of Jacob, are not consumed." God does not change! Do you believe the God of the Old Testament is the same as the God of the New Testament? Of course you do! So God does test us, that we may be perfect and complete, lacking in nothing.

Whoever you are, whatever the circumstances of your life, the way you respond to all of these tests and temptations will determine whether you have the crown of life. One exciting difference between God's tests and most tests a student takes in school is that with God, if you flunk, He says, "I'll tell you what—I'll let you retake the test." God wants you to pass every test!

We have come full circle to James 1:2-4: "Consider it all joy, my brethren, when you encounter various trials, knowing that the testing of your faith produces endurance. And let endurance have its perfect result, that you may be perfect and complete, lacking in nothing" (*NAS*). This is the way God works. This is the theology of life: an overall view of the way you can look at every single circumstance, small or large, that happens to you from now until the Lord returns!

It's the devil who wants you to yield to anger and bitterness, resentment, hate and impurity. Let's lean the other way. Instead, yield to love, kindness, forgiveness, a tender heart and heart purity. Pass the tests; be crowned with life.

When you are tested, is it the devil? Is it God? Always both. You are in the middle, and you are the one who makes the choice. Anything that happens to you is always both a test and a temptation. You determine whether you are defeated or become "perfect and complete, lacking in nothing." The choice is your responsibility.

Chapter Nine

Encouragement: A Way Of Life

There was a famous psychologist from Harvard, now deceased, who wrote a book that has become somewhat of a classic. His name was William James. In this book, he reports on his studies of the spiritual experiences of people. He determines that the number one need in the life of every human being is to feel appreciated. Isn't that interesting? The number one need that both you and I have is for someone to come along every day and say, "Hey, you're neat," to encourage us.

The Bible has some very important things to say about encouragement. "Take care, brethren, lest there be in any one of you an evil, unbelieving heart, in falling away from the living God. But *encourage* one another day after day... lest any one of you be hardened by the deceitfulness of sin" (Hebrews 3:12-13, *NAS*). This verse actually says that the opposite of encouragement is the hardening of our hearts to *sin*. To say it in another way, the reason people harden their heart is because no one has encouraged them. No one has come along and said, "Hey, friend, you're going to make it. Just hang in there and keep believing. Just let me encourage you."

Have you considered that backsliding is the opposite of encouragement? I wonder how many young people there are today who are in the world, living in sin because their mom or dad didn't encourage them, didn't put their arms around them and tell them they were loved and appreciated? I wonder how many Christians there are who have been so beat down as to be set up for the enemy because no one encouraged them to keep believing?

The Bible says to encourage one another daily. Do you realize that everyone around you needs to be encouraged on a daily basis? Your husband needs encouragement. Your wife needs encouragement. Your parents need encouragement. Your children need encouragement. Your boss needs someone to encourage him. Your employees need to be encouraged, and we need someone to encourage us, too.

Now that you're catching the spirit of this chapter, let's just look at that scripture from Hebrews again: "Take care, brethren, lest there should be in any one of you an evil, unbelieving heart, in falling away from the living God. *But encourage one another day after day,* as long as it is still called (Today), *lest* any one of you be hardened by the deceitfulness of sin."

Note the word *lest* in that passage. Encourage one another *lest* you be hardened. We all need encouraging. Then the devil comes along and says, "If we encourage so-and-so, they'll get all puffed up and proud." But that's a lie from the devil. The Bible says that the devil is the accuser of the brethren. The devil specializes in negativism and condemnation. But the Spirit of God is the opposite of condemnation. The Spirit of God is encouragement. You're not going to puff somebody up by telling them you appreciate them. Say to your wife, "You know what? You make the best cinnamon rolls in the nation." Now, actually, my wife makes the best cinnamon rolls, but you go ahead and encourage your wife, too. How long has it been since you went to your dad or your husband and said, "I really appreciate the fact that you work hard to provide for us and keep food on the table?" It really does something within you when somebody encourages you. In fact, encouragement discourages sin. Encouragement discourages a hardened heart. The opposite of the deceitfulness of sin is daily encouragement.

Think for a minute about the teacher that you liked most in school; or think about the pastor or friend that you enjoy the most—that has blessed and helped you most. I know which one it was. It was the one who most encouraged you.

I can remember a Vacation Bible School teacher I had. I can't remember a thing she taught me, but she patiently helped me put a little butterfly decal on a flower pot to give to my mother, and I'll never forget that woman. She was an encourager to me. When I think about pastors, a brother comes immediately to mind. He shows up a couple of times each year with his little ukulele and a permanent grin on his face.

You know, he can go any place and within half an hour everybody is so encouraged and blessed that they don't want to sin. We need to adopt encouragement as our way of life, something we are called to do.

Dwight L. Moody once said, "I have never known God to use a discouraged person." That's quite a statement.

There is a story that has Satan auctioneering off his tools. He was willing to part with everything except one little sledge hammer. When the devil was asked why he was not willing to give up that tool, he said, "That is the spirit of discouragement, and I am not willing to part with it."

I looked up the word "encouragement" in the Greek and found that it occurs 142 times in the New Testament. In the King James Version, it is often translated as "exhort." I used to think of the word "exhort" as a negative word. When someone said, "Brother, I have a word of exhortation for you," in my mind's eye I could see a shotgun, and the speaker was putting a shell in each barrel, cocking it back and ready to shoot. I always wanted to respond, "Thanks, but no thanks. I'm busy now. Could I see you later?" However, I know now that exhort is not a negative word. It means "to encourage." The Greek word is *paraclete*. The verb is *parakaleo*. It means, "one called aside to help." It's the name given to the Holy Spirit. Jesus said, "I will send you another paraclete"—another helper, another comforter. In John 15:26, Jesus says, "When the comforter comes"—or when the encourager comes—not the clobberer. So this word, in Greek, means "encourager." When you see the word "exhort" from now on, think of the word "encourage."

Look at the word "encourage." Break it apart—*en-courage*. It means to "put courage into." If I encourage you, I put courage into you. If you are going through a trial, and I tell you, "Hang in there and keep on keeping on till you turn that trial into victory," I am putting courage into you. That's encouragement. That's a powerful word.

Every Christian is called to be an encourager. When Thomas Edison was inventing the light bulb, he failed hundreds of times. When somebody asked him, "Did you fail again?" he answered, "That wasn't a failure. That was an education." He had a spirit of encouragement, a spirit of faith.

In Matthew 5:4, Jesus says, "Blessed are they that mourn: for they shall be comforted." The Greek word for "comforted" means "encouraged." So blessed is the person who is sensitive, who can cry, who can understand the needs of others, because they are going to be encouraged—infilled with courage. Selfish or unfeeling people are often depressed, but "Blessed are those who mourn, for they shall be encouraged."

There's more encouragement to be found in Hebrews concerning church attendance. Hebrews 10:23-25 says, "Let us hold fast the confession of our hope without wavering, for He who promised is faithful; and let us consider how to stimulate one another," (the King James Version says 'provoke one another.' Yes, we are good at provoking one another, but the passage is better translated as 'stimulate one another') "to love and good deeds, not forsaking our own assembling together, as is the habit of some, but encouraging one another; and all the more as you see the day drawing near" (*NAS*).

He says we are coming into the last days, so go to church and encourage one another, build each other up. One of the purposes of church is to encourage each other.

In Acts 4 the Scriptures speak of a man who was such a special brother that the apostles changed his name. In verse 36, it tells of a Levite named Joseph, "who was also called Barnabas by the apostles (which translated means 'Son of Encouragement')." The Greek word used there is paraclete. How would you like someone to say of you, "That sister's name should be 'Daughter of Encouragement'"?

The Bible tells us to encourage one another daily. That's our job. It's our God-given task. If we don't do it, we're not following the Lord's instructions to us. We are not only to encourage each other day by day, but we are to make encouragement a way of life.

Another description of Barnabas as an encourager is found in Acts 11:22-23, which says, "And the news about them reached the ears of the church at Jerusalem, and they sent Barnabas off to Antioch. Then when he had come and witnessed the grace of God, he rejoiced and began to encourage them all with a resolute heart to remain true to the Lord"

(*NAS*). Barnabas was truly an encourager.

Paul was an encourager, too. Acts 14, beginning with verse 6, relates the story of Paul, along with Barnabas, in the city of Lystra. If you don't know that story, read it. It's a startling and encouraging short episode in Paul's life. After a lame man was healed, the people began to worship Paul as a god. When Paul denied this acclaim, Jews came from neighboring cities, and incited the crowd to stone Paul and leave him for dead outside the city walls. But God raised Paul up from the stoning, and he and Barnabas went to another city for a short revival meeting. Then, they went right back to Lystra where Paul had been stoned, strengthened the souls of the disciples, encouraged them to continue in the faith, and said, "Through many tribulations we must enter the kingdom of God" (Acts 14:22).

When Paul was stoned and left for dead, he didn't feel sorry for himself. He went right back to that same town and encouraged the believers. What would you and I have done?

Again, in Acts, chapter 20, it talks about encouragement. This scripture tells of the time when Paul preached all through the night. There was a young man by the name of Eutychus sitting on the third story window sill. He went to sleep during Paul's lengthy sermon, thereby assuring that his name would be remembered through all succeeding generations. Eutychus dozed and fell out the window, and was picked up dead.

Verse 10 says, "But Paul went down and fell upon

him and after embracing him, he said, 'Do not be troubled, for his life is in him.' And when he had gone back up, and had broken the bread and eaten, he talked with them a long while, until daybreak, and so departed. And they took away the boy alive, and were greatly comforted" (*NAS*).

The Greek translation says that they were greatly encouraged. In the margin of my Bible, it explains, "They were not moderately encouraged." In other words, they had a hallelujah, hollering, praising time! They really got encouraged. Well, if someone died and was raised from the dead in the middle of one of my lengthy sermons, I'd be more than moderately encouraged, too!

Romans 12:8, speaking about the gifts of the Holy Spirit, tells us that if our gift is to be an encourager, then encourage. Now you know that the Bible says that we should earnestly seek the best gifts. Well, I believe that one of the best gifts we could have is to be an encourager, to practice encouraging people day by day.

Let me encourage you with another scripture. In just five verses of Second Corinthians, chapter one, the Bible uses the Greek word "encourage" ten times. Now, the New American Standard Version translates the Greek word in this passage to say "comfort." But it is the same Greek word which means "encourage" or "encouragement."

Second Corinthians 1:3-7 says, "Blessed be the God and Father of our Lord Jesus Christ, the Father of mercies and God of all *comfort*; who *comforts* us in all our affliction so that we may be able to *comfort* those who are in any affliction with the *comfort* with which we ourselves are *comforted* by God. For just as the sufferings of Christ are ours in abundance, so also our *comfort* is abundant through Christ. But if we are afflicted, it is for your *comfort* and salvation; or if we are *comforted,* it is for your *comfort*, which is effective in the patient enduring of the same sufferings which we also suffer; and our hope for you is firmly grounded, knowing that as you are sharers of our sufferings, so also you are sharers of our *comfort*" (*NAS*).

Substitute the appropriate form of the word "encourage" in place of the word "comfort" in the above passage, and it will encourage you. Paul is saying that all those trials you have suffered will serve to prepare you to encourage somebody else who is going through the same trial. You may have lost a loved one. That is a hard trial. But in it, you find that Jesus is sufficient and that you are now qualified to comfort and encourage someone else who has lost a son, daughter, parent, wife or husband. The Bible tells us that trials will prepare us to become encouragers.

Second Corinthians 2:7-8 says, "On the contrary, you should rather forgive and comfort him, lest somehow such a one be overwhelmed by excessive sorrow. Wherefore I urge you to reaffirm your love for him" (*NAS*).

Understand the context of this passage. There was a man in the Corinthian church who was committing adultery with his stepmother, and the church had ex-communicated him. That is a pretty gross sin. But Paul said that since he had repented of his sin, the church should now encourage him, or the man might be overwhelmed by his guilt and sorrow, even though God had forgiven him. When a person has repented and turned from sin, he needs to be encouraged and loved.

There was an artist who started his career with a job as a staff artist on the Kansas City Star newspaper. But the editor was displeased with his work and said to him, "Young man, why don't you get into a profession you are qualified for?" The editor fired him. But another man encouraged this young artist. He said, "Draw me a picture of my horse, and I'll give you a dollar." This young man became a world-famous artist because somebody encouraged him when he needed encouragement. His name was Walt Disney.

As a youth, O. J. Simpson, the famous running back, was placed in a home for juvenile delinquents in Chicago. Someone asked Willie Mayes, the baseball star, "Would you take one hour and go visit a young man in trouble in a juvenile home?" Well, Willie Mayes did, and he spent an hour with O. J. Simpson in the home—and O. J. says today, "When Willie Mayes left, I knew that I could get it together." Because someone encouraged him, that young man became a professional football star.

Did you know that Abraham Lincoln failed in business in 1831? But not only that. He was also defeated as a candidate for the legislature in 1832. He failed again in business in 1833; suffered a nervous breakdown in 1836; was defeated for Congress in 1843 and again in 1848; defeated for the Senate in 1855; defeated for Vice president in 1856, and defeated again for the Senate in 1858. But, he was elected President of the United States in 1860!

Old Abe kept trying, didn't he? Somebody must have encouraged him. If I had been so beaten down, had a nervous breakdown, failed in business twice, lost nearly every election, I think I might have given up after awhile. But somebody encouraged him. And the Lincoln Memorial stands in Washington, D.C. today, quietly proclaiming the success of that encouragement.

There are many more scriptures on encouragement that could be quoted, but I want to go back to the first scripture I used in this chapter, to the one that says, "Encourage one another *day after day*...lest any one of you be hardened by the deceitfulness of sin" (Hebrews 3:13). Now, if you are convinced that encouraging each other daily is a good, desirable, and scriptural thing to do, then I want you to do the following six things:

First, simply make the decision right now that encouragement is going to become a way of life for you. Determine right now that you are going to live that way, that encouragement will become a part of your character. I really encourage you to make that decision right now!

We have a man in our congregation who is an

encourager. He just encourages everybody. It's a gift. It's an anointing on him. I have seen him in crisis situations where most people would have rebuked somebody, but he encouraged them. When a person gets completely off track and goes off on a tangent, the average leader would say, "You're off the track and taking too much time. You're dominating the group. Why don't you just cool it?"

Do you know what he would say? "You know, I want to thank you for your comments. That's really helpful, and we're going to pray about it. I appreciate you."

This is the way God wants us to live. Grab everything that is negative and turn it around to the positive. Be the encourager. Look for what's good in every person and latch onto that quality instead of criticizing and beating them down. The "weirdest" person has some beautiful characteristics.

Do you want to be appreciated and well-liked? Make a definite decision to make encouragement a way of life for you. It will take experience. You won't always do it perfectly. But work at it. God will use you as an encourager.

Second, when we encourage a person, we need to be specific. Encourage them about a particular thing. Instead of saying, "That was a fine sermon," you need to say, "That point about being faithful really helped me, and I appreciate it." I know that when someone encourages me, I preach better.

Third, be sincere. Actually look for the attribute or characteristic of a person that you can sincerely encourage them about. It's not difficult to spot a phony. Be natural, be normal, and be sincere. Don't be so overly-spiritual or so heavenly-minded as to be no earthly good. And if somebody gives you encouragement, why not just give them a hug and say, "Thanks, I appreciate that."

Fourth, send notes. I'm serious. I know that postage stamps are more expensive than they used to be, but it's more than worth it. I've been trying to do that. I have a little notepad that says, "From the Pastor's desk." I just write a short note to people when they come to mind. "Hey, I appreciate you. I appreciate your faithfulness." It comes in the mail totally unexpected, and that person is built up and encouraged.

Then, there are people in our congregation who will just occasionally send me a card in the mail, saying something like, "Thank you for being my Pastor." It really makes my day. It truly encourages me. It is the opposite of sin. "Encourage one another daily... *lest* any one of you be hardened by the deceitfulness of sin."

Determine that you are going to be a blessing to others. It will help and encourage you. It's the opposite of accusing the brethren. It's the opposite of gossip and slander.

I think you ought to send a couple of notes each week. It only takes a minute or so.

When I was in Holland, I found that European people have a custom. Every Friday afternoon, as a man comes home from work, he buys a flower and takes it to his wife or sweetheart or mother. You see flower vendors on almost every corner on Fridays. They don't spend a lot. They don't buy a dozen roses. They buy one tulip, or one daisy, or whatever, and they take it and say, "Here. I love you." That is a beautiful custom. It's the same thought as sending a note. It shows appreciation, and it encourages the receiver.

Fifth, be people-conscious. Be aware of people. Be aware of relationships. The older you get, the more you understand that what really counts in life is people, not "things." The key to life lies in how you treat people.

Jesus said, in Luke 12:15, "A man's life consisteth not in the abundance of the things which he possesseth." Life is greatly enhanced by friends and relationships, so be aware of the people around you. Be people-conscious.

Sixth, right now, make a mental list of three people that you are going to encourage this very day. It's not enough to obey the Scriptures tomorrow. The Word says, "Encourage one another day after day, as long as it is still called 'Today.'"

Right now, you have probably already thought of at least three people that you could encourage today. So do it! Make up your mind that when people see you they will say, "There is an encourager."

Now, let me encourage you in the most important encouragement I can give: If you are not saved, if you haven't received the born-again experience, then I urgently encourage you to get saved today.

Don't finish this book without receiving Jesus Christ as your Lord. Pray this prayer from your heart now:

"Father, I have sinned against You and Your holy Word. But I believe that Your Son, Jesus, became a man, was crucified, buried and rose again so that even I could be saved from my sin. I repent of my sins, and I turn from them now. Forgive me, Father, and send Your Holy Spirit to live in me and guide me into righteousness. Thank you, Father, that I am now born-again. I believe I am forgiven and that You are now in me. I believe I am now saved. I confess You, Jesus, as my Lord. Amen."

I encourage you. If you are not certain that you have ever prayed a specific prayer such as the above, then do it right now—with all your heart. It's so simple, so easy to do. Yet your eternity may depend on your having prayed just such a prayer.

Again, if you have salvation, but have not experienced the baptism in the Holy Spirit, I encourage you greatly to seek and ask, and receive this infilling that your Lord Jesus wants every Christian to have. He wants to give you this gift that will fill you, encourage you and embolden you. It will bless you beyond all you can think or expect, and it will empower you to live in victory in every area of your life! It will give you all the freedom you need to grow in God's love and grace!

"Now may the God of hope fill you with all joy
and peace in believing, that you may abound
in hope by the power of the Holy Spirit."
(Romans 15:13)

ABOUT THE AUTHOR

Ernest J. Gruen, currently, is the pastor of the Full Faith Church of Love, in a suburb of Kansas City. The Full Faith Church of Love is a spirit-filled, inter-denominational church that has become a teaching center for the midwest. In its 16 year history, the church has grown from an attendance of 25 to the present 2500 attending on Sunday mornings.

Pastor Gruen is the son of a devout American Baptist deacon. He was converted at age 9 and called into the ministry at age 19. He then received the Baptism in the Holy Spirit at age 29. He served as an American Baptist pastor for 10 years. He received his BA degree from Friends University (Wichita, Kansas), where he graduated with honors; and has a Master's of Divinity from Central Baptist Theological Seminary in Kansas City.

He has been married to his wife, Delores, for 27 years, and they have four grown children. Their oldest daughter, Michelle (25), is a registered nurse, working on her master's degree. Their second daughter, Renee (24), is currently ministering and living in Jerusalem, Israel. The next two children are twins, age 22. Mike is an employee of the U.S. Postal Service, and Cheryl is a chemical engineer, doing drug research.

Ernest Gruen's previous book, *Freedom to Choose,* is in its fifth printing and is also published by Whitaker House. Pastor Gruen speaks extensively throughout the midwest at churches, colleges, and Full Gospel Businessmen meetings. He especially enjoys ministering in seminars on a variety of subjects.